The Search for Me

The Search for Me

A Bible Study by
Kristie Kerr

ISBN: 978-0-578-08199-1

Printed in the United States of America

1st Printing

Contents

To my three beautiful daughters:

My enduring prayer for you is that you would live your lives with confidence, grace and assurance.

May you know and fully embrace all of the stunning layers of who God made you to be.

And may you find your identity completely in Him.

Acknowledgements

There is a special group of women to whom I owe a huge debt of gratitude for the contents of this book. The River Valley Moms have been my friends, my inspiration and my muse for almost nine years. I miss you terribly, but I continue to write with your faces in my mind and your voices in my heart.

Thank you to Carol Hollen for once again using her amazing eye for detail in helping me edit this book. Thanks for being a smarty pants. And for letting me borrow your beautiful brain.

Dena Swenson – an email from you automatically meant squeals and giggles from me. Thank you for sharing your amazing talent for all things lovely and beautiful with me.

To my dear, dear friend Carol Lund. I'm sure there are better encouragers in the world than you – but I have yet to find one. Thank you for breathing confidence into me. I truly want to be you when I grow up.

To my amazing friends who constantly support and stand beside Jeff and me. I never realized how RICH our lives were until we faced a new adventure and felt the arms of so many loved ones holding us up and cheering us on. We are overwhelmed with your kindness.

To Amber Bertsch for listening to Jesus and filling a HUGE need in my life. You DO NOT KNOW how much you continually bless me.

To John & Ruth – as the years go by, I am more and more inspired by the life of faith you live. Thank you for loving us and being such a vast well of wisdom for Jeff and me. We love you.

To my sister and brother, Kate & Rick. You have absolutely blown me away by your unwavering belief in me and the dreams I have in my heart. Thank you for pushing me forward and standing beside me along the way. Let's "git er done."

Mom & Dad – Well. I'm not sure what to say. You love me, help me, inspire me, support me, listen to me, and tell everyone you know about me. What more could a girl ask for? I love you.

Lucy, Charlie, Betty & Dottie - You're my favorites. Forever.

And to my sweet, sweet Jeffrey. I couldn't be more proud to be forever attached to you. Thank you for taking me on a great adventure.

Introduction

I. Love. Women.

I think we're collectively a pretty fantastic idea.

I believe in us. I believe in our potential to be a monumental force to show a hurting world the kindness of our Savior.

But we will never be effective in that call until we overcome the baggage and weight that most of us are carrying around: a crippling lack of confidence and identity.

That is why I wrote this study.

My prayer for you is that you would dive in, do the hard work and let God point out areas in your heart that need to be healed, confessed and set free. Let Him replace your self-sufficiency with a dependence on Him. Allow Him to give you an impenetrable sense of identity and confidence – and then go change the world.

This book is designed to be used in many different ways. You can go through the lessons by yourself, in a small group or large group setting. There are group discussion questions at the end of each chapter to initiate connection and growth within your groups. The "Going Deeper" section is a place designed for you to spend time contemplating each topic, examining your own heart and allowing God to speak truth and direction to you.

If you are using this for a large Bible Study, feel free to teach the material by extracting the main points and then adding your own personal stories and insight. Many of you have God-given leadership and teaching gifts… use them! Even if you're scared or unsure, take a step and give it a try. You'll be surprised how God will use you if you'll give Him the opportunity.

I'm praying for you. May God do a great work in your heart.

You are SO loved.

Kristie

What About Me?

MY LIFE AND PURPOSE

Eventually, each of us recognizes the need to know who we are.
— "A Woman's Identity" by Elaine Stedman

It was 2004. I had just given birth to my third child. My oldest had just started kindergarten, which was an emotionally traumatic experience in and of itself. And the "organizational demands" that accompanied me sending my little princess into the world of picture days and sharing topics were completely overwhelming this mama. I was volunteering countless hours at my church and found my duties there multiplying and expanding faster than I could keep up. My house was a mess. My car was a disaster. My emotions were shot and my husband was concerned.

I was driving in my car on my way to the "millionth" appointment one of my kids had, when a lovely little song by one of my favorite singers came on the radio. Tears streamed down my face as I listened to Keith Urban sing these words:

I'm living in a world that won't stop pulling on me.
I know it sounds crazy, but it's true;
It's like I owe my time to everyone else,
And that's all I seem to do.
Sometimes I can't help thinking, "What about me?"
Some days go by that I don't even see;
I'm doing everything right, and I can't break free.
Is this the way it's always going to be?
"What about me?"

What About Me
by Keith Urban

And I asked myself that very question! "What about me?!?" I was madly in love with every role I was playing in my life: mother, wife, volunteer, employee and many, many other things. But, I felt like I had lost a sense of "me." It was as if my personal identity had become absorbed in my daily duties and roles. I knew what my jobs were – but was that the extent of who I was? Somewhere lost in the middle of all I had to do, I couldn't remember what it was that I **liked** to do. I didn't know how to get it back … and I wasn't sure I was "allowed to."

Even asking the question felt wrong! A huge sense of guilt washed over me for even entertaining the thought. Was I just being self-absorbed? Only thinking about myself? I'm sure there are moments when I was just being a big baby and was frustrated that I couldn't have everything the way I wanted it, but deep down I felt like the question was much more significant than that. If I didn't figure out how to pour myself into all these things without losing my sense of personal identity, I knew that there could be serious repercussions to the very things I held so dear to my heart.

Have you ever felt that way? That your life is just happening TO you? You're not fully present, but simply reacting to the next thing on your list? It's as if you're not really LIVING your life, your LIFE is living you. You look in the mirror and don't recognize the person looking back at you. You're lost inside your own life, and not sure how to find your way back?.

I just felt out of touch with my life, like it was ahead of me, always slightly out of my reach. I was chasing it rather than leading it, and catching up only from time to time.

Coming Up for Air by Margaret Becker

At one time or another, all of us face a sense of not knowing who we are. We may know all the roles we play, but we're not sure if that is all we are. We can be passionate about the jobs we have: wife, mother, employee, boss, friend, daughter, volunteer – and still have a lack of understanding about our personal sense of identity. At times, all our roles become consuming, and we feel like there is no room left for us as a person.

So I began to search for answers:

- What is my identity?

- How do I take ownership of my life?

- How do I fulfill all my roles and yet maintain my identity?

- How do I remain ME in the midst of all the things around me pressing me to be something I'm not?

- There are thing I don't like to do, but I have to do them. How do I find passion for these things?

- How do I maintain a sense of self – and yet give myself fully to my family, friends and job?

- How do I not let my life pass me by – but be fully engaged and creating the life God has designed for me?

- Is it okay for me to want all these things – or am I just being selfish?

When we have lost our sense of identity, one of two things will typically happen: We either will become DEPENDENT or RESENTFUL.

If we become DEPENDENT:

- We pour more and more of ourselves into our jobs, our kids, our spouse, our homes--hoping to find our identity IN them.

- We live vicariously through others' experiences and emotions, and therefore have no real sense of personhood or boundaries.

- We become dependent on others for our affirmation, our confidence and security.

- We turn into a doormat.

- We don't truly own our lives; we are letting others live it for us.

- We find ourselves at the mercy of other people because we are so completely dependent on them to feel validated.

If we become RESENTFUL:

- We get cranky and self-centered.

- We start getting agitated by the needs of our family, friends, bosses and spouses.

- We begin to put the focus on what WE want first, and then everyone else gets what's left.

Lesson One

- We start to keep score, only giving what is equally returned.

- We build walls, staking our claim on what's mine, without a sense of concern towards others.

- Our frustration at the things needing our time and energy can cause resentment to overflow and may lead to destructive life choices.

So, of course, there's only really one thing to do when faced with an identity crisis … and it's NOT getting a nose ring and skinny jeans! I RAN to Jesus. Not walked – RAN to Him. I had to get real and honest about where I was and what I was feeling. I had to fall on my face before Him and ask Him the questions that I desperately needed answered. And of course, He is always so faithful to give insight and direction to us when we come asking the hard questions.

Here are some of the things God spoke to me about my identity:

1. He created me as a unique person … and I should be me.

    a. God specifically formed everything about me.

- He's given me a personality.

- He's given me desires.

- He's given me passions.

- He's given me intellect.

You made all the delicate, inner parts of my body and knit me together in my mother's womb. Thank you for making me so wonderfully complex! Your workmanship is marvelous—how well I know it. You watched me as I was being formed in utter seclusion, as I was woven together in the dark of the womb. You saw me before I was born. Every day of my life was recorded in your book. Every moment was laid out before a single day had passed.

Psalm 139: 13-16

God created everything about you! The way you think, the things <u>at which you are gifted</u>, the way you see the world. He hand-selected all the delicate, intricate parts of your personality and intellect. Your gifts are no accident; they were specifically given to you before you were formed, to equip you to accomplish the purposes that God has for your life. What a wonderful thought!

So why, oh why, do we spend so much time trying to be something we're not?!

    b. We constantly compare ourselves to others and then feel lost when our lives don't mirror the people around us.

- We discount the value of our gifts because we don't think they're as good as those of our friends.

- We are discontent with our home, spouse, career and finances because they don't look like the homes, spouses, careers and finances of those around us.

- Or worse yet, we are frustrated and unhappy because all of those things don't look like the picture we envisioned in our hearts and dreams, and so we decided to make huge, destructive life choices out of desperation – trying to find our identity in something or someone new.

- We lose sight of who God made us to be, and can only see the things we are not.

I recently pulled some jeans out of my closet that I hadn't worn in awhile. As I pulled them on, I realized that I was – perhaps – a tad … hmmmm … how should I put this … more rotund than the last time I had tried on said jeans. But I was determined to wear them. So I jumped and squirmed and pulled until I got them on. I started my schedule of activities but constantly found myself uncomfortable and distracted. I felt "off" the entire day.

There is nothing more frustrating than trying to wear something that doesn't fit. When you are searching for your identity, and trying and become something you are not – you are going to find yourself frustrated and unfulfilled because you are trying to be something you were never created to be.

It's like the story of David in 1 Samuel 17 where David is going to go out and fight Goliath. Saul, the King of Israel, offers David his armor to wear into battle. As David puts on the heavy helmet and coat, he realizes that he can hardly move in the weighty armor. In verse 39, he says, "I can't go in these," he protested. "I'm not used to them." He realized that Saul's armor was made for Saul. And if he was going to fight this giant, he was going to have to do it being himself. He didn't need to fight as an armor-bearing soldier, he needed to go as a sling-throwing shepherd. Thankfully, David recognized this before he stepped out into the battle wearing something that didn't fit him.

Lesson One

> *You will never find your identity as long as you are trying to be something you were never created to be.*

The second thing I learned about my identity is:

2. It's okay for me to have boundaries where my family and job ends and I begin.

   a. It is SO easy to get lost inside of our roles.

   b. We can get swallowed up in everyone else's needs and expectations for us.

   c. It is OKAY to have things you enjoy just for *you*!

   d. It is HEALTHY for you to have your own sense of personhood.

   e. We tell ourselves that we are being selfless but truly we are robbing the people around us a healthy version of us.

   f. It is not healthy to be selfish and indulgent – but it also is not healthy to neglect taking care of yourself and tending to your own person and needs.

Oh my – the guilt we face as women! I feel guilty if I go out and do something just for myself. I feel guilty if *I DON'T* do something for myself. I feel guilty when I have to say no. I feel guilty when I say yes. I am learning that guilt is *NOT* my friend. Because it's not based on the reality that *I NEED* to make space for myself in my life: I need to do the things that make *ME* feel like *ME*. I will be a better mother, wife, daughter, friend, employee and volunteer when I have taken the time to nourish my own body, mind and soul.

We constantly need to be replenishing ourselves. We keep pouring out and pouring out, and eventually there is nothing left to pour out. And the fundamental, first and foremost place we have to go to be replenished, is at the *feet of Jesus*:

- Spending time reading the Bible: Letting its truths comfort us, challenge us, and fill us up.

- Spending time praying: Simply talking to God about where we are, our needs, concerns and hurts. And then listening for Him to whisper to our souls words of wisdom, direction and affirmation.

- Spending time in worship: Honoring God for who He is, gaining perspective as we acknowledge His faithfulness, sovereignty and power.

- And after we've gone to Jesus to fill us up, we can do lots of practical things to refresh and replenish our minds and bodies. It doesn't have to be a big ordeal or expensive--or even all that difficult!
- Lock the door and read a book in the bathtub.
- Go out for a cup of coffee.
- Get outside and go for a long walk.
- Have a "Skype date" with a friend at the end of a long week.
- Rent a movie and make a big bowl of popcorn.
- Spend half an hour in a store you love just walking around, looking at things that inspire you.

Another lesson I learned in my search for identity:

3. It is vitally important to the people in my world that *I know who I am*.

   a. A strong sense of identity leads to:

- contentment;
- balance and lack of over commitment;
- freedom from people pleasing.

   b. Knowing who you are frees you to serve others and brings glory to God.

In John 13, we find the story of Jesus washing His disciples' feet.

Jesus knew that the Father had given him authority over everything and that he had come from God and would return to God. So he got up from the table, took off his robe, wrapped a towel around his waist, and poured water into a basin. Then he began to wash the disciples' feet and to wipe them with the towel he had around them.

John 13:3-4

In Jesus' day, it was a customary gesture when you entered someone's home to have your feet washed by a servant. They walked long miles on dusty roads in sandals, so their feet were definitely in need of some attention when they arrived at their destination. We don't know exactly what happened in this situation, but for some reason this (foot-washing) custom had been overlooked.

I can imagine, all the disciples sitting around wondering, "Who is going to wash everyone's feet?" I'm sure the inner dialogue was interesting. "I'm not doing that, that is someone else's job!" Or "What will everyone think of me if I wash everyone else's feet?" Or perhaps, "Well, I've been a disciple longer than HE HAS so *HE* should be the one to wash feet."

But, Jesus KNEW who He was. He knew what the Father had sent Him to do. He was not concerned with His image, the way other people saw Him, or trying to promote Himself. Because He was confident in who He was in the Father, He had no problem serving those around Him. His security allowed Him to fulfill any role asked without the baggage of insecurity.

> When you KNOW who you are in Christ, you will be able to freely give to others without dependency or resentment.

Lastly, my search for identity taught me:

4. **The only way to "find myself" is through laying down my own ideas and taking on HIS identity for me.**

   a. I had to stop asking myself the question "who am I?" – and begin asking God "Who did You make me to be?"

   b. Instead of figuring out what I wanted to do, I began asking God what HE wanted me to do.

   c. I had to let go of my preconceived ideas, agendas and expectations; I had to lay down everything … and trust that He would fill my heart again with His plans and purposes for me.

   d. I began to look at all the things about me through *His* eyes with *His* purposes in mind for my life.

- My personality: Why did He create my personality this way?

- My interests: What things fill me with excitement? What am I good at doing? How would I spend my time?

- My outlook: What is my general perspective on life? What things am I passionate about? What things am I *NOT* passionate about?

When I seek God and take on His identity for me, I will find that it is totally "me" because He *created* me. I find I can be totally "balanced" because He never asks me to do more than I can with His help. With God's identity, I can be totally "unselfish" because I am truly concerned about *HIS* plans and not *MY* plans.

Dependence is replaced with Confidence;
Resentfulness is replaced with Servanthood.

So this really is a trust issue. It goes against my human reasoning to think that the way to get back a sense of identity is to lay down every hope, desire and want; I have to trust that the true life He has for me will be fulfilling, abundant and more "*me*" than anything I could ever try and create on my own.

If you try to keep your life for yourself, you will lose it. But if you give up your life for me, you will find true life. —Matthew 16:25

Humility happens to us when we least expect it and when we are least aware of it. It is the by-product of a realistic appraisal of who we are before God, the appropriate acknowledgement of our needed dependence upon him. It is the absence of egocentricity, or self-focus; it is seeing ourselves and others from Christ's point of view. It is the attitude which motivates us to set aside our self-centered ambitions and desires in deference to God's work in both our lives and others', giving precedence to God's plan rather than our own. It is an affirmation of who we truly are: God's own person, in whom neither conceit nor self-deprecation is appropriate. —A Woman's Worth by Elaine Stedman

So, ask yourself, "Am I willing to go on this journey with you, Lord? If I give you access to every part of my life, will you help me find myself again? Will you lead me on this journey?"

Are you tired? Worn out? Burned out on religion? Come to me. Get away with me and you'll recover your life. I'll show you how to take a real rest. Walk with me and work with me – watch how I do it. Learn the unforced rhythms of grace. I won't lay anything heavy or ill-fitting on you. Keep company with me and you'll learn to live freely and lightly.

Matthew
11:28-30
MSG

GROUP DISCUSSION QUESTIONS:

- Why do you think it is so easy to lose our identity as women?

- Are you more prone to become *resentful* or *dependent* toward your family, job and others in your life?

- Do you find it hard to spend time and energy on yourself? Why do you think that is the case?

GOING DEEPER

It is so easy for us to lose our sense of identity and find ourselves lost inside our duties and roles. Some of the questions we discussed earlier were:

- What is my identity?

- How do I fulfill all my roles and yet maintain my identity?

- How do I remain ME in the midst of all the things around me, pressing me to be something I'm not?

- How do I maintain a sense of self – and yet give myself fully to my family, friends and job?

Take a minute and write out some of your own questions in your search for identity in the space provided.

Lesson One

When we finally get honest with our feelings and frustrations, there is nothing more important than to bring all of those things to God. It can be tempting to run *FROM* Him, assuming that He would be disappointed in us. Or we walk away, blaming Him for the position in which we find ourselves. But the only place to find our true identity is in Him.

Take a few minutes right now and *RUN* to Jesus. Pour out your heart to Him. **Write out your most deep, honest and scary feelings. Ask Him to meet you here and begin to give you the answers you need.**

We all want to satisfy "me." But why are there so few satisfied "MEs" around? Part of the problem lies in the lack of structured boundaries within our personality. We can't define who the real "me" is and what we truly desire.

Boundries by Dr. Henry Cloud & Dr. John Townsend

Nothing will make you more dissatisfied with your life than trying to be something you're not. **Be honest with yourself as you answer the following questions.**

In what areas of my life am I trying to be something I'm not?

To whom am I comparing myself?

Where are you finding yourself lacking contentment? Is your discontentment coming from trying to make yourself wear something that doesn't fit?

God grants us an uncommon life to the degree we surrender our common one.
—Cure for the Common Life by Max Lucado

It is so important that you take care of yourself. Figure out what replenishes your heart and mind, and be diligent about making it a part of your regular routine. **Write out a few ideas here.**

It is vitally important to the people in your world, that you have a strong sense of identity. Confidence, balance and service all begin when we know who we are in Christ.

Self-care is the acceptance of personal responsibility leading toward getting filled mentally, physically and emotionally. It begins with recognizing the truth of who you are – your identity and value in God. This process enables you to become and remain a full vessel, and then to give from your abundance. Self-care is about wholeness.

The DNA Relationships for Couples by Dr. Greg Smalley & Dr. Robert S. Paul

How do you think your lack of personal identity is affecting the people in your life?

How would your relationships change if you had a strong sense of who God wanted you to be?

Lesson One

Spend some time praying. Ask God the following questions:

- Who did You make me to be?

- What are the things YOU want me to do?

- Why did you create my personality this way?

- What are my interests? What am I good at?

- What things am I passionate about? What am I NOT passionate about?

Come to me. Get away with me and you'll recover your life. –Matthew 11:28

What Do I Want?

UNDERSTANDING OUR DESIRES

The desire of a woman's heart and the realities of a woman's life seem an ocean apart. —"Captivating" by John & Staci Eldridge

Desire is a pretty tricky thing. The word is used in many contexts, but most of them refer to something forbidden or out of balance. And it's true: Desire can be all consuming; it can overcome our reason and our sensibility; it is a powerful force.

But desire isn't necessarily bad. Actually, I would venture to say that desire is good! We can define the things we truly care about by looking at our desires. It exposes things in our hearts and minds. Good desires--healthy desires--are the things that keep us in touch with the core of who we are and what is important to us. Even bad desires--those that are rooted out of selfishness and unhealthy motive--can be helpful to us. They can be red flags that something is not right. The intensity of a sinful desire can lead us to repentance and right living if we take the desire and recognize its destructive nature and bring it to the feet of Jesus.

But whether good or bad, you've got to be willing to recognize your desire. There are times that our desires scream out to us with everything in our being; there are times that they are hidden beneath layers of obligation and duty; I have experienced both.

Recently, I discovered my dream house. Oh my, oh my. It's a beautiful Queen Anne-style estate, built in 1875, tucked away in a quiet neighborhood a few minutes from my house. It has huge, old windows; a quaint patio covered by big, aged trees that are just screaming for a tire swing. It has ornately carved banisters and more history and charm than I can hardly handle. I. Want. That. House.

I drive by it all the time. I look it up online. I took a bunch of pictures and secretly look at them a few hundred times a day. I. Really. Want. That. House.

Problem is, my husband: He. Really. Does. Not. Want. That. House. When he looks at this house he does not see the same quaint sanctuary that I see--he sees a money pit. He doesn't want anything to do with a 130-year-old building. He sees unending remodeling projects and hidden costs … and huge headaches. I think he is convinced it's going to fall over any minute.

So, we're at an impasse. But my desire continues to grow stronger and stronger for my little house. So what do we do? Nothing. We just wait and try not to fight about it. I find myself getting extremely frustrated and upset. I find myself feeling very misunderstood and defensive. And I find myself struggling. I completely love and respect my husband and trust that he has our family's best interest at heart; he wants what is best for me and for our children. But my desire could convince me otherwise. It could lead me to believe that this home is worth a division in my marriage. It could lead me to become resentful that my husband doesn't see things the way I see them. It could cause big problems.

So, I keep bringing my desire to Jesus. Daily I lay it at His feet. I pray that He will take away selfishness and give me an eternal perspective. I ask Him to help me honor my husband. I pray for wisdom as to how to negotiate this disagreement in my marriage. Desire has led me to a state of surrender to which I must continually return each and every day.

In other seasons of my life, I have been completely disconnected from my desires. A few years ago, I was speaking at a women's event at our church, and they asked me to make a list of five of my favorite things to use as giveaways for the ladies attending the service.

I sat down to make my list and couldn't think of a single thing that I liked. I was shocked with how disconnected I was from the things that I enjoyed: I realized that catering to my wishes was a luxury I had long neglected. What did I eat for lunch today? Whatever the kids ate. What did we eat for dinner? Whatever was handy. What did I do when I had an hour to myself? Go to the grocery store so I wouldn't have to take the kids with me the next day. I never even thought about what I would enjoy. The mundane tasks of my everyday routine had quietly, but systematically, taken over any thoughtful intention towards my desires. I did not have the time or energy to think about what I wanted, I simply just had to "git 'r done."

And as disconnected as I felt from my everyday wants, I was even more unaware of the big life desires in my heart:

- What do I feel passionate about?
- What would I love to do?
- Where would I love to spend my time?
- What are my disappointments?
- Where do I feel like I am failing?
- What would l love to have God heal in my life?
- What do I long for in my personal relationships?
- How do I want my career and ministry to look?

In this chapter, we're going to look at the two-sided coin of desire: The importance of being in tune with what is going on in our hearts so we don't walk through our lives without purpose and direction ... simply reacting to things around us without a sense of direction and connection. And the other side of desire: Working through the strong and powerful force that desire can be in our lives. Refusing to allow it to lead us down paths of destruction by continually surrendering every desire to Jesus.

First, why do you think so many of us are disconnected with our desires?

1. Busyness

    a. We have so many "needs," there is little time for what we discern to be our "wants."

    b. We have very little time to rest, think and reflect on our longings.

    c. We are racing through list after list, appointment after appointment, going from one thing to another, and we never stop and think about the things we are doing.

- Are we *REALLY* doing all these things because they are valuable and important to us, or are we simply doing what we think we're "supposed" to be doing or what everyone else is doing?
- Are we filling our lives so completely full that we have no time to reflect?
- Are we simply reacting to the needs of those around us instead of purposefully and systematically making our lives what God wants them to be?

    d. We simply are so busy that our life is a blur of activity that is not at all connected to our desires.

Lesson Two

Another reason we are disconnected with our desires is....

2. Fear of disappointment

If I'm really honest, I think that part of the reason I don't think about what I want is because I fear the disappointment that comes from not being able to have that desire being met. It's really a self-protection thing: If I don't think about what I wish for, then I can't be let down when I can't have it.

    a. We would rather keep our deepest desires at bay, than to actually hope to see them fulfilled and be disappointed.

> *Sacred Rhythms by Ruth Hayley Barton*

Worse yet, what if I touch that place of longing and desire within me and let myself really feel how deep it goes, only to discover that those desires cannot be met? What will I do with myself then? How will I live with the desire that is awake and alive rather than asleep and repressed?

    b. Maybe you have hoped for things in the past and seen those hopes not come to fruition. So you shut off the place in your heart that leads to your desires because it's just too painful.

There is a story in 2 Kings 4 of a woman who had given up on her desires. This woman has welcomed the prophet Elisha into her house. She has graced him with hospitality and kindness, and in return, he asks her if there was anything he can do for her. Her answer is "no." But upon further inquiry, Elisha discovers that she has no heir. So, he prays to God, and she is given a child.

I find it interesting that she didn't ask Elisha to pray for her to become a mother. Elisha was a well-known prophet. She must have been aware of the high profile, high impact miracles that God had done through him. And, for a woman in that time in history, not only was there real heartache from not having a child, there were social consequences for a woman without an heir: The family name would cease; her land and possessions would pass on to others. Children were a woman's only source of security in old age after her husband died. Why would she not ask for a miracle baby?

When Elisha speaks the words of healing to her, "Next year at about this time you will be holding a son in your arms." (2 Kings 4:16), her response is not what you would expect: She says, "No, my lord! Please don't lie to me like that, O man of God!" What made her react in such a negative way? What made her heart sink with anxiety?

I can only imagine the journey that had brought this woman to such a place. Perhaps there were years of infertility; perhaps she had lost children; perhaps she had suffered miscarriages. I have a dear friend who endured three painful miscarriages in a short span of time and the grief she experienced in not only losing those precious babies, but the heart-wrenching disappointment of not becoming a mother, was almost too much to bear.

My heart tends to think that her response to Elisha was one of self-protection. I think what she meant to say was, "*PLEASE* don't tell me something that isn't going to happen! I cannot bear to think that I might actually have a child, and then be disappointed again." She had lost hope.

Later on in the story, after her son is born, he becomes ill and dies. As she rushes out to meet Elisha we hear the truth of her heart: "It was you, my lord, who said I would have a son. And didn't I tell you not to raise my hopes!"

There it is--the truth of her response: She was kicking herself for actually believing that she was going to get her happy ending; she was frustrated at the man of God for opening up her sealed heart and allowing her to dare to dream of a future with her child. It's almost as if she is saying, "I KNEW it was too good to be true." It hurts to hope and be disappointed.

Hope deferred makes the heart sick.... –Proverbs 13:12

Lesson Two

Another reason we are disconnected with our desires is....

3. Guilt

    a. It feels self-indulgent to focus on ourselves.

- We feel guilty when we take the time to focus on what *WE* want.

- We ignore our own needs and simply focus on the needs of everyone around us instead.

- It is definitely God honoring to serve others, but Jesus regularly got away for time to hear from the Father.

Immediately after this, Jesus made his disciples get back into the boat and head out across the lake to Bethesda, while he sent the people home. Afterward, he went up into the hills by himself to pray.

Mark 6:45-46

    b. It feels arrogant to name ambition.

- We have all been around people who are completely consumed with their own wants and agendas and I think it's natural for us to be nervous about becoming "one of those people."

- But we have to understand that there is a huge difference between narcissism and self–awareness.

- I believe the more you seek God for *HIS* identity for you, the less "self-absorbed" you become; you become more and more focused on *HIS* desires.

    c. We confuse humility with disengagement

- God desires for us to be fully present in the life He has given us.

- We must be sensitive to the Holy Spirit speaking direction and discernment to our hearts, and we cannot do that if we have shut the door.

Another reason we silence desire in our life is....

4. We're just too tired

    a. When you feel completely depleted emotionally, physically and spiritually, it is difficult to gain any sense of personhood.

    b. It takes too much effort when you feel like you are already expending more energy than you actually possess.

    c. Taking initiative for yourself can seem overwhelming when you're already exhausted.

Then Jesus said, "Let's go off by ourselves to a quiet place and rest awhile." He said this because there were so many people coming and going that Jesus and his apostles didn't even have time to eat.

Mark 16:31

And the last reason we silence desire in our lives is....

5. Fear of bad desires

a. "What if I get in touch with what I want and it leads me into sin?"

- We are afraid to let ourselves open up totally for fear that our flesh will take over.

- This is a very valid concern, and something not to be taken lightly.

- We must sort through all our desires and own what is fleshly and sinful and bring it to Jesus, asking Him to help us sort through all the things in our heart.

Lesson Two

Many desires masquerade as the real thing. They are lusts that come out of not owning our real desires.
—*Boundaries* by Dr. Henry Cloud and Dr. John Townsend

James 1:14, 15

Temptation comes from the lure of our own evil desires. These evil desires lead to evil actions, and evil actions lead to death.

b. "Maybe it's better to keep it all locked up, than to risk letting the bad stuff out."

- The solution is not just to keep all desire closed up and out of reach.
- The solution is to bring every thought to Jesus, and surrender everything to Him.
- He knows everything about us anyway … we are not hiding anything from Him.
- It is only when we bring the darkest parts of our lives into the light of His presence, can we find freedom from sinful desires that would lead us down a destructive path.

He reveals the deep things of darkness and brings utter darkness into the light.
—Job 12:22 NIV

Why should we get in touch with our desires?

1. Our desires are the core of who we are.

    a. They reveal what is most important to us.

- Our hopes for the future

- The fundamentals of how we want our lives and relationships to look

- The mark we want to leave on the world

- What is valuable to us

As I spent more and more time praying about my "dream house" situation, I took the time to go beneath the surface and determine what was at the core of my obsession. Did I just want a bigger house? Was I being superficial and materialistic? As I dug deeper, I realized that much of my desire for this house was a reaction to a season of extreme busyness from which Jeff and I were just emerging. I was tired of both of us working so much, and deeply longing for more family time and investment into our personal lives. I saw this house as a chance to spend time together fixing it up. I envisioned us in our paint clothes, putzing away on a Saturday afternoon while we turned this old shack into a beautiful home for our family. I was also feeling a sense of adventure growing inside of me and a longing to do something new and exciting. Little did I know that just a few months after I discovered this house, that God would lead my husband and I to quit our job and begin a new venture and launch a new ministry. Once I realized what was at the core of my desire, it helped me to release the specifics (like... I *HAVE* to have this house or I'm going to *DIE*!!!!!) and realize that there were plenty of other ways I could make these core values a reality in my life. I'm thankful that I kept surrendering it to Jesus and that I was able to look beyond the superficial reasons I wanted to move, and tap into the really important stuff behind it. (By the way ... someone else bought my dream house. I'm somewhat over it, although I still occasionally drive by ☺)

    b. If something is significant to you, your desires will reflect that core belief.

- Example: If your relationship with girlfriends is fundamentally important to you, you will desire to spend time with them. You don't have to *MAKE* yourself want to go out to lunch with your friends, you *WANT* to. Your desires reflect what is significant to you.

- You will know what is meaningful to you by your desires

Another reason we should get in touch with our desires….

2. Our desires will expose the condition of our heart

    a. In 2 Chronicles 1, we read the story of Solomon, the son of King David being named successor of his father's throne. After all the ritual and ceremony had taken place, Solomon is anointed King of Israel. He honors God with sacrifices and commits to lead the people in a Godly manner. His leadership is pleasing to God, so one night God comes to him in his sleep.

> *That night, God appeared to Solomon in a dream and said, "What do you want? Ask, and I will give it to you."* –2 Chronicles 1:7

Can you imagine being in that moment? Can you imagine if God Himself tells you that you can ask Him for *ANYTHING*, and it will be given to you? I'm sure Solomon felt the gravity of the moment. When he answers God, his response is simple: He asks for wisdom and knowledge in order to lead his people well. Once again, his response is pleasing to the heart of God.

> *God said to Solomon, "Since this is your heart's desire and you have not asked for wealth, riches or honor, nor for the death of your enemies, and since you have not asked for a long life but for wisdom and knowledge to govern my people over whom I have made you king, therefore wisdom and knowledge will be given to you. And I will also give you wealth, riches and honor, such as no king who was before you ever had and none after you will have.*
>
> 2 Chronicles 1:11, 12 NIV

b. Solomon's desire exposed the condition of his heart:

- He wanted to honor God in the position he had been given.

- He wasn't concerned with being wealthy or famous or renown; he simply wanted to do what God had asked of Him.

- His heart of service and leadership was revealed through the naming of his desire.

c. When we honestly look at our desire, we will see a true reflection of our motives.

- Areas that are motivated by selfish gain and are egocentric in nature.

- Areas that are motivated for Kingdom purpose.

- Areas of our hearts that are surrendered to Jesus.

- And areas of our heart that are *NOT* surrendered to Jesus.

God gives gifts to His children, but He is a wise parent. He wants to make sure His gifts are right for us. To know what to ask for, we have to be in touch with who we really are and what are our real motives.

Boundries
by Dr. Henry
Cloud & Dr. John
Townsend

Lesson Two

Another reason we should get in touch with our desires....

3. Our desires shine a light on the areas of our life that are out of alignment.

If you take the time to figure out what your desires are, you then can look at every area of your life and make an assessment as to whether or not your actions actually reflect those core values.

    a. Ask yourself: Where am I spending my energy?

- If you determine that one of your greatest desires is to see restoration in your marriage, then you can begin taking steps toward healing your marriage.

  1. Getting counseling.

  2. Making appropriate changes in your attitude and behavior.

  3. Cutting back on work hours or extra activities to make time to spend with your spouse.

- If you determine that raising healthy children who love God is one of your greatest desires, then you can orchestrate your lives and schedules around that core desire.

  1. Making your home a place filled with faith and open conversations about God.

  2. Prioritizing relationships and activities that teach them about God and scripture.

  3. Prayers at bedtimes, honest talks at the dinner table, healthy correction, and discipleship are all prioritized in the home that is committed to raising kids who love Jesus.

    b. Ask yourself: Where am I spending my time?

- Does it reflect my desire and core values?

- Am I wasting time on things that don't really matter to me in relation to the things that truly hold significance for me:

  1. Spending a lot of time with your face in your phone or computer, instead of spending quality time with your children?

  2. Giving an out-of-proportionate investment in volunteering while your family is feeling isolated from you?

  3. Focusing too much time on your job, and the relationships in your life are suffering for it?

- If you took a hard look at where you spend your time, is it reflective of the things God has called you to do?

Maybe God has put on your heart that you need to be sharing your faith with people who don't know Jesus. Yet your over commitment at church keeps you from spending any time with friends, neighbors or co-workers who don't have a personal faith. This is a sign that you need to make some changes and decisions as to how you are spending your time.

    c. Ask yourself: Where am I spending my money?

- My Dad always taught me that one of the easiest ways to determine the things that are of value to you is to look at your bank account.

1. Where are your finances going?

2. Are they reflecting the things that are close to your heart?

3. Are you being generous?

4. Are you being frivolous?

5. Are you honoring God with your money?

6. Or is your checkbook reflecting an out–of-balance desire for things and status and significance?

I had to stay with my longings in His presence and get honest about the ways my life as I was living it was not congruent with my heart's deepest desires. This was a stunning realization; after all, I had made most of my own life choices. How had I ended up here?

Sacred Rhythms
by Ruth Hayley Barton

Lesson Two

We also should be in touch with our desires because....

4. We cannot just ignore our bad desires; we need to acknowledge them, confess them, and pray for strength not to succumb to them.

a. Dark things love the dark.

b. Secrets are a breeding ground for destruction and sin.

God's light came into the world, but people loved the darkness more than the light, for their actions were evil. All who do evil hate the light and refuse to go near it for fear their sins will be exposed. —John 3:19-20

c. When we have thoughts, intentions, and desires that are not God's best for us, it is vital that we bring them into the light so that we ruthlessly can deal with them before they have a chance to grow.

d. Truthfully assessing your hidden motives and thoughts and bringing them to Jesus is profoundly important in your spiritual walk.

e. When we acknowledge our temptations, they lose power over us. When we confess and repent to Jesus, HIS supernatural power kicks in to give us strength to do the right thing.

I have a dear friend who is not married. An old boyfriend of hers contacted her a few months ago, and began to tell her how unhappy he was in his marriage and how he really wanted her back. YIKES! My friend was trying to be strong about the whole situation, but this guy knew the keys to her heart and preyed on her loneliness. Being the wise, godly woman that she is, she sent out an S.O.S. She contacted me, asking for prayer and accountability. She didn't IGNORE what was going on in her heart. She ACKNOWL-DEGED that she was being tempted by her feelings. She CONFESSED that she was struggling and asked me to PRAY with her for strength to do the right thing.

Her willingness to be honest about her desires allowed me to pray with her, and also set up some accountability between the two of us. Every Monday we talk and she lets me know if she has had contact with this guy. (Who is STILL trying to contact her even after she told him to leave her alone ... grrrrrrrr.) We share scriptures that strengthen her resolve. We pray together. We do not allow these desires to sit in the darkness – but we continually bring them into the light together and surrender them to Jesus.

Another reason to be in touch with our desires....

5. Our relationship with Jesus grows deeper as we share the deepest parts of our heart.

    a. Something significant happens when we name our most intimate desires.

- We feel known.

- We feel understood.

- We feel close to the person who knows such intimate things about us.

- I remember when Jeff and I first started dating and we would sit up all night long talking about *EVERYTHING*. What we wanted to do with our lives. How we wanted our family to look. Our deepest fears and grandest hopes. Something amazing happened in those late-night talks: Our hearts were knit together and our desires started to become one cohesive unit.

    b. When we share the deepest parts of our heart with God, our desires begin to be shaped and synchronized with HIS plans and desires.

I love this verse in Psalms:

Take delight in the LORD, and He will give you the desires of your heart.
–Psalm 37:4

Unfortunately, sometimes we think that this verse means that God should give us everything our heart wants. That doesn't really make sense, because we all know that the desires of our hearts aren't always in alignment with what He has planned for us. And that kind of faith will leave you disappointed and frustrated because God simply isn't a vending machine where we put in our quarters of investment and He just magically produces our craving of the moment.

What I have come to understand about this scripture is this: As I delight in the Lord--as I spend time with Him, learning about Him, surrendering myself to Him--I find that the desires of my heart become conformed to His plans and purposes for me; I no longer want the selfish and simple things my heart *USED* to think it wanted. My desires become His desires; my deepest hopes are His purposes and plans for my life. I change. I grow. I evolve.

c. We simply must come to Him with every desire and lay them before Him.

- The good, the bad and the ugly.
- There is no safer place to lay our every desire than at the feet of Jesus.
- The Bible is full of honest, raw, emotive cries to God.

I am exhausted and completely crushed. My groans come from an anguished heart. You know what I long for; you hear my every sigh. –Psalm 38:8

d. We don't need to edit ourselves with God.

- He knows every thought and desire.
- He is not shocked or offended by our honest assessment of our desires.
- The safest thing to do with any and all desire is to continually, openly and honestly, bring them before God and ask Him to continually conform our desires into HIS desires.

e. Intimacy is birthed out of honesty and vulnerability.

- Opening up the deepest part of your heart to God is a very important part of our spiritual journey.
- Having that very sincere and honest dialogue with Jesus helps you grow closer and closer to Him
- The more time you spend with him, the easier it is to hear and recognize His voice and follow His leading.

I remember so vividly a summer where I was feeling just a nagging feeling in my heart. My oldest daughter, Lucy, was five; my son, Charlie, had just turned four; Betty Ann was one.

And I wanted another baby.

This might not seem like such a big deal, but for us this was an *ENORMOUS* decision. Charlie was born prematurely, and had faced countless obstacles and struggles in his short time on earth. He was doing really well, and we were profoundly grateful for the hand of God in healing and restoring him. But my pregnancy with Betty had been *INCREDIBLY* stressful. The doctors had no idea what had caused Charlie's early arrival and therefore the smallest little thing would send us rushing to the hospital to make sure everything was alright. It was such a difficult season for both of us.

But I wanted another baby.

I found myself sitting on a bench in front of a lake having some quiet time with Jesus. Logic told me that I should be thankful to have three healthy babies – that in and of itself was a miracle – and not to push our luck. I didn't know if we could handle another nine months like that again. I was trying to reason myself out of what I knew what going on in my heart.

But as I sat on that bench praying, I heard the voice of God very clearly whisper to my heart. I heard him say, "Kristie, what do you want?" I am REALLY good about articulating all the things I *SHOULD* say ... but honestly to look inside the deepest part of my desire and voice my truest longing was actually quite difficult for me to do.

I finally said, "Jesus, I really want another baby." There was such a sweet release that happened in that moment. To name my deepest desire in His presence ... just the two of us ... was so very intimate. Just to be able to be totally honest. Not having to edit yourself, but just laying it all out there.

In that moment, I knew that if it wasn't His will for us to have another child, that He was going to help me lay down that desire. And if it was His plan, that He would be with me every step of the way. All the anxiety and discontentment I had been feeling melted away and I just felt peace about the whole situation.

Almost a year to the day later, I learned I was pregnant with our sweet Dottie. And that little girl is the embodiment of *JOY* in my world. I often think of the moment I cried out to God for her. What a treasured memory.

Psalm 21:2
NIV

You have granted him the desire of his heart and have not withheld the request of his lips.

Lesson Two

And the last reason we should be honest with our desires....

6. God-given desire gives birth to God-directed action.

    a. God's presence is the safest place in the world to discover your dreams.

- The most fulfilling and rewarding part of being in touch with your desires is the ability to shape your life to include these things.

- You can become purposeful about being involved in things that are directly related to your passions.

    b. When we get in touch with our gifts and passions, we can begin to dream about how God can use those passions.

    c. We can discover the next steps we should be taking.

- Maybe you need to take a leap of faith into a new career or ministry.

- Maybe you should go back to school and develop skill in your area of passion.

- Maybe you should simply change your life to allow more time for the things to which you are deeply connected.

May he give you the desire of your heart and make all your plans succeed.
–Psalm 20:4 NIV

As I peel away the layers of my desire, I allow God to work in the deepest part of my life. He helps me diffuse the ones that could harm me; He ministers to the ones that are wounded. He helps me organize my life around the things that I am passionate about. And when we go through this process together, I feel His companionship and sovereign direction in my life.

I desire to do your will, my God; your law is within my heart."

Psalm 40:8
NIV

GROUP DISCUSSION QUESTIONS:

- How connected to your desires are you right now? Are you in a season where the deep parts of your heart are locked away and hidden? Or are you dealing with a desire that is in the forefront of your life?

- Think of a very strong desire from your past. Was it healthy or unhealthy? How did you deal with it? What was the outcome of that situation? Share you experience with the group.

- If you're comfortable, share something you are currently desiring in your heart and life. Share your thoughts and spend time praying together over this specific issue.

GOING DEEPER

Okay, here we go: It's time to spend some time connecting with what is really at the core of your heart and life. Time to go to the core of who you are and allow yourself to be really honest, truthful and vulnerable about your deepest desires. It's vitally important that you don't edit yourself. **Lay it all out there. Jesus will help you sort it all out – but you must be honest.**

"What do you want me to do for you?" Jesus asked him.
–Mark 10:51

Lesson Two

Jesus repeatedly asked people in the Bible this question. Now He is asking you: What do you want Him to do for you? Write out your thoughts here.

Sometimes we are afraid to ask for something because we don't want to be disappointed if it doesn't work out. Express your fears and apprehensions here.

Here are a few more areas of desire to explore. Answer the following questions:

What do I feel passionate about?

What would I love to do?

Where would I love to spend my time?

What are my disappointments?

Where do I feel like I am failing?

What would I love to have God heal in my life?

What do I long for in my personal relationships?

How do I want my career and ministry to look?

Perhaps your desire is leading you down a path that isn't God's best for you. Confess that here and ask Him to give you three steps of wisdom as to how you can flee this temptation. **Write out those steps here.**

Write out Matthew 26:41.

Write out 1 Corinthians 10:13.

Looking at your desires, make an assessment of where you are spending your time, energy and resources. Is it reflective of your core desires? List some specific changes you could make to allow your "real life" to line up better with your core values.

Now that you've identified your God-given desires, take some time thinking of some God-directed action. **Let yourself dream big and then list some practical steps you can take to begin seeing these dreams become a reality.**

She is clothed with strength and dignity, she laughs without fear of the future.

−Proverbs 31:25

Lesson Two

Major Meltdown

Dealing with Burnout

My friend was exhausted. "I'd throw in the towel," she joked, "if I could just find it – and had the energy to throw it." —*Mommy Burnout* by Rebecca Prewett

"I think I'm having a breakdown. I'm not sure where you're supposed to go when you have one, but I think that's what this is."

This was the conversation I had with myself as I drove around aimlessly one cold Minnesota night a few years ago. Hours earlier I had impatiently put my children to bed after a long day of laundry, diaper changes and homework. Then the phone rang and I spent an hour on the phone with someone discussing the best method to launder the tablecloths at church. (No kidding.) I couldn't remember the last time I had slept an entire night, and finally the evening culminated with a "meteoric explosion" aimed directly at my shocked husband. I'm pretty sure I said some words that would embarrass a sailor. Not my finest moment.

As I drove around, I was beside myself. Who in the world was this person? This was not me. I would love to say that this was the first time this kind of emotional outburst had happened, but it was becoming an all too regular occurrence. I found myself in a place where I just didn't seem to be able to cope with my life. I was exhausted. I was anxious. I was overwhelmed. I was impatient. The smallest thing would leave me in tears.

What was I going to do? I was mortified to think that I was not strong enough to be a good mother. I was mortified that I was such a horrible wife. I couldn't imagine there was ANY way I could live up to the expectations I had put on myself for church commitments. I felt completely trapped and had *NO* idea what to do next.

I drove back home and blubbered out a huge apology to my ever-so-calm husband. He graciously forgave me and then said, "Honey, maybe you just need to get away for awhile." Within two days I was on a plane to Nebraska to visit my grandma. I spent four or five days in her QUIET house just reading, praying, SLEEPING and trying to get some perspective.

Oh, what a huge blessing those days of rest were for my weary, weary soul. And that was just the beginning of my journey back. I had to make some significant changes in my life. I bought a little pillow on that trip that still sits on my sofa. It says: SIMPLIFY – and that's what I began to do. I cut out a lot of extra commitments. I let go of some of my "superwoman" pride and asked for help when I needed it. I even decided to let go of my part-time job teaching piano lessons, which was a huge financial decision for our family. It took awhile, but I found myself in a much better place emotionally, physically, and spiritually.

In this day and age where our lives move at insane paces, our responsibilities are compounded and there is little room for silence and rest, burnout is an all too common occurrence. Stress, anxiety and over commitment are regular parts of our lives. And the by-product of our over commitment is that many of us are walking around on the brink of collapse.

Psalm 40:11, 12

Lord, don't hold back your tender mercies from me. My only hope is in your unfailing love and faithfulness. For troubles surround me – too many to count. They are more numerous than the hairs on my head. I have lost all my courage.

In this chapter we're going to talk about:
- What burnout is and what causes it.
- How to recognize when you're on the road to burnout.
- How to recover from burnout.
- How to put things in place so you don't burnout again.

So, what is Burnout?

Burnout is a state of emotional exhaustion. It can manifest itself in many different ways, but it is usually accompanied by feelings of being overwhelmed, stressed out and fatigued. It is a response to prolonged stress and emotional overload. And over time, if you continue feeling this way, it can segue into apathy; you feel helpless to change your circumstances, and therefore you stop even trying. You may find yourself disinterested, unmotivated or unproductive.

Basically, your mind and body cannot keep up with the emotional and physical demands on it, and it begins to shut down. Burnout is your mind and body's way of saying, "HELP!"

It is much more protective than destructive. It instantly slows you down and produces a state of lethargy and disengagement. The system gives out before it blows up.

−*Depressed, Stressed, and Burned Out: What's Going on in My Life?* by Dr. Archibald Hart

What are some symptoms of burnout?

- fatigue
- irritability
- emotional outbursts
- self-criticism
- apathy
- disillusionment
- disengagement
- lack of motivation
- physical symptoms including headaches, backaches and stomach problems
- decreased satisfaction in your life and work

How did I get here?

1. Physical Reasons:

    a. Serotonin is the chemical in your brain that makes you feel good about life. Sometimes your body is depleting the supply faster than it can replenish it.

- Some things that deplete serotonin include the following:
  - lack of sleep
  - constant state of busyness and work with few breaks
  - lack of exercise
  - absence of activities that replenish you
  - stress
  - poor nutrition

- Some things that increase serotonin levels include the following:
  - sleep
  - sun
  - exercise
  - any kind of meditative activity (prayer, resting, friendly conversation)
  - providing your body with a lot of healthy, vitamin-rich foods

If you feel your burnout is severe, don't be afraid to talk to your health professional. Sometimes doctors will prescribe medication that can raise your serotonin levels in addition to these natural therapies.

    b. Too much "Fight or Flight"

Do you remember learning about this in your junior high human biology class?!? The fight or flight response is the body's natural way of dealing with stress. When our minds perceive danger or a high stress situation, your brain releases SUPER chemicals and hormones to help you deal with the situation. It gives your body excessive strength to be able to fight your adversary OR run away quickly. When you hear of moms lifting cars off of their trapped children, the fight or flight response is in effect.

- The problem for us is that most of the "stress and danger" we face in our everyday lives is less likely to involve the lifting of cars. We feel anxiety and stress, and our bodies release these chemicals; then we don't actually burn away the excess by "fighting or flight-ing." The chemicals build up in our bodies and can cause wear and tear on our minds and bodies.

When the system is constantly subjected to this emergency response and when there is nothing to fight or flee from, the body adapts to this state by producing complex stress hormones from the adrenal glands that cause an increased state of wear and tear in the body.

Depressed, Stressed, and Burned Out: What's Going on in My Life? by Dr. Archibald Hart

c. Hormonal changes

Let me start by saying this: I've never been one of those girls who blame everything on her period. Yes, we all have to deal with hormonal things, but using it as an excuse has always … well … just bothered me. BUT! I also have learned to recognize the fact that, as women, we are created WONDERFULLY COMPLEX and there are very real hormonal changes happening in our bodies all the time that can affect our attitudes and emotions.

- Our hormone levels change when we ovulate, have our periods, are pregnant, just had a baby, get older, get even OLDER and for any number of other physical reasons.

- It's important to be aware that these things definitely can factor into how we are feeling physically and emotionally.

I remember when Jeff and I first got married, I was taking birth control pills and the combination of hormones made me pretty much *HATE* my husband. (Pretty effective form of birth control!) I talked to my doctor, got the dosage figured out and got back to my normal, loving self. But it was a good eye-opener for me to be aware that there could be very real *PHYSICAL* reasons for *EMOTIONAL* symptoms.

- Now, this isn't an excuse to say, "Well, I'm hormonal, so I'm just going to behave however I want to!!" But learn to identify those triggers, and use it as a red flag to be more careful with your words and more mindful of your actions. There are some days I just know to keep my mouth shut and stay out of everybody's way. And if it's becoming a serious problem, it's okay to talk to your doctor about solutions to get your hormones in balance.

- **SPECIAL NOTE:** If you have just had a baby, and are feeling blue for a prolonged period of time, you could be suffering from post-partum depression. Don't mess around with it; go talk to your doctor and get some help.

Lesson Three

d. Lack of exercise

There are people who like to exercise … and there are people who do *NOT* like to exercise. I am of the latter persuasion; I'm not one of those people who when they have an hour to themselves thinks, "You know what would be SO much fun...running five miles." However, I *KNOW* that I feel better when I **MOVE**.

- We all know that lack of exercise can cause weight gain and other physical problems; but we also need to realize that it can have emotional effects on us too.

- Countless studies and unending research shows the connection between our physical activity and our emotional health. Exercise has been proven to improve mood levels, reduce anxiety and help fight depression.

e. Eating habits

- Our bodies need good fuel to run properly.

- When we fill our bodies with junk, they don't have anything to run on.

- Too much sugar, too much caffeine, too much of everything (or anything) can cause our bodies not to operate well.

A body system exhausted by overwork, pushed beyond reasonable endurance, and depleted of resources could become burned out.

—*Depressed, Stressed, and Burned Out: What's Going on in My Life?* by Dr. Archibald Hart

2. Emotional Reasons for Burnout:

a. Relentless emotional strain:

- caring for ailing or elderly family member

- stress at work

- caring for children

My own personal season of burnout definitely was caused in part by my family situation. Lucy was five years old and had just started kindergarten, which was a HUGE adjustment for this mommy. I wasn't used to having my family on a schedule (we're a pretty laid back crew) and it was a really hard change for me. Charlie was four and was struggling with some speech and motor skills; I was taking him to private therapies four times a week on top of Early Childhood Special Education classes. However the crazy schedule was nothing compared to the emotional strain of worrying about my son. And then there was Betty--she was around 18-months old and was into E-V-E-R-Y-T-H-I-N-G! My other kids had been so easy compared to her, and I just couldn't seem to keep her out of mischief. Looking back at it now, I can see why I was so stressed out!

- financial problems
- marital issues
- conflict
- death or loss
- any other emotional strain that continues over a long period of time

  b. Change:
  - new job situation
  - moving to a new house, neighborhood or state
  - adjustments to new season of life with kids
    - new baby coming into family
    - kids starting school
    - toddlerhood, Tweens, Teenagers
    - empty nest
    - becoming grandparents
  - Change in a personal relationship
    - romantic Breakup
    - loss of friendship
    - conflict with a relative

c. Isolation:

- changes in work environment where you are no longer with peers/friends
- choosing to stay home with your children and your contact with the "outside world" is significantly altered
- increased travel by you or your spouse causes more and more time alone.
- embarrassment over personal, financial or marital troubles can cause you to withdraw and isolate yourself
- over commitment in activities causes disengagement from life-giving relationships

d. Worry:

- anxiety over finances
- concerns for children and other family members
- apprehension for the future

e. Tremendous mental fatigue of trying to wear a lot of hats

- having to be too many things to too many people
- being spread too thin
- the constant pouring out of yourself for everyone else's needs leaves you empty and depleted
- having little or no personal time to be replenished

How do I get out of this?

1. Honestly evaluate your life and circumstances.

a. What is out of control?

- Look at all areas of your life and make an honest assessment of your health in these areas:
  - relationships
  - health. (diet, exercise, rest, controlling health issues)
  - spiritual health
  - work situation
  - pace and level of activity

- expectations. (example: Perfectionism can raise your anxiety level and cause an enormous amount of stress.)

- causes of stress and anxiety

b. What do you need to accept that you cannot change and let go of?

• You cannot change other people.

• Sometimes you cannot change your circumstances and you need to learn how to exist *within* them.

When you get down to it, there are *VERY FEW* things that you cannot change. You cannot make people do what you want them to do, but you *CAN* change your reaction to them. You cannot "undo" a bad thing that has happened to you, but you *CAN* be diligent about moving towards healing and restoration in Jesus. You may not be able to change the way your boss treats you, but inevitably you *CAN* quit your job. I think many times we think we are powerless to change things, when in reality, we are *AFRAID* of changing them. True, you cannot change everything, but I have made a decision in my life in the last few years not to be a victim of my own life: If something isn't working, there usually is *SOMETHING* I can do to change it; even if it's changing myself to adapt to a difficult situation.

c. What can you change?

• You can change your diet.

• You can get more exercise.

• You can get more rest.

I recognize that there are seasons of life that can cause us to have less time for sleep. I remember those days so well, when I was up all night … every night; and I remember the toll that it would take on me physically and emotionally. It's so important during those times to be strategic about finding times to rest. I was pretty religious about napping when my baby napped. And when I had older kids too, and that wasn't always an option, Jeff and I would make sure that we took turns caring for the kids and getting plenty of naps.

And now that my kids are older, I find the greatest threat to me getting enough rest is *ME*! I stay up late putzing around on Facebook, surfing the Web, watching TV, or generally wasting time. For me, now it's more of a self-discipline issue to make sure that I go to bed at a decent hour and get enough rest every night.

> *It's useless to rise early and go to bed late, and work your worried fingers to the bone. Don't you know He enjoys giving rest to those He loves?*
> —Psalm 127:2 MSG

- You can control the pace of your life and how many extra activities in which you and your children are involved.
    - sports
    - extracurricular activities
    - volunteering at church
    - how many nights a week you have activities outside the house
- You can seek help for marital and relational problems.
    - Seek counseling.
    - Read books and articles on relational issues.
    - Join a support group.
    - Consistently pray for the people in your life and ask God to give you wisdom and insight.

After you've evaluated your life, the next step is to….

2. Make changes.

    a. Look at the list above and recognize some of the things that you can positively do to affect your emotional and physical health.

    b. Commit to making those changes.

    c. Do *SOMETHING*.

- Sometimes just taking control of one thing can play a huge part in restoring a sense of hope.
- Even if you're not entirely successful in your efforts, just taking the step forward is so important.

    d. If you can't make changes for yourself, do it for your family.

When I was pregnant with Betty, I spent eight weeks on bed rest. I was stuck on the couch with a house that was dirty, two other kids that needed parenting and a husband with a full time job. People were offering to come and help me with housecleaning, bringing meals and babysitting. At first, I refused all their offers because I didn't want to put anyone out and thought that we could do it ourselves. But a friend told me something that changed my perspective dramatically. She said, "I know it's hard to accept help. So if you can't do it for yourself, do it for Jeff and the kids. *THEY* need you to let me help you."

Sometimes it's hard to make changes for ourselves; finding the motivation to tackle daunting challenges can be very difficult. But I've found that sometimes I am far more inspired to make changes for those I love. I don't want to be a "cranky-pants" with my kids all the time because I'm spread too thin. So that can motivate me to drop some of the extra activities to make more time for my family. I want to be fun and energetic with my husband, so I can make some changes to my personal care to make sure I have a better outlook and disposition. At the heart of the matter, you need to make changes for yourself, but sometimes the push you need to get started will be motivated out of a desire to be a healthier version of you for the people you love.

Another way to help fight burnout, is to...

3. Take a break.

    a. Every day....

- Rest when you can.

- Plan for times to take care of yourself throughout the day.

- Start and end your day with time for reflection.

- Do one thing every day just for you.

    b. Every week...

- Honor a Sabbath.

- Do something you enjoy.

- Engage in a hobby that relaxes you.

  - Spending time with people who replenish you.

  - Reading books that inspire you.

  - Go to a place that brings you joy.

  - Playing, creating and relaxing should be a regular part of your weekly routine.

Lesson Three

- Have a Night out.
  - Get dressed up.
  - Go out and have fun with your friends or your spouse.
  - Remember what it's like to be a person: not just a mom, wife or employee.
- Find "your time."
  - Determine a weekly time for you to replenish yourself.
  - Maybe every Sunday night you to paint your toenails and mentally prepare yourself for the upcoming week.
  - Maybe you and your husband take turns sleeping in on Saturday mornings while the other one watches the kids – so each of you gets some extra rest.
  - Maybe you have a weekly date with a local coffee shop where you spend an hour journaling, writing letters and thinking.

We Kerrs don't have many routines, but there is one weekly ritual that almost always happens: Every Monday morning my husband goes out for an hour or two by himself. This all started when we first got married and we were music pastors at a church. We soon discovered that the weekends were extremely draining for both of us, but especially for Jeff. He's more of an introvert, and the emotional energy he put forth at church just really took it out of him. So we learned that he just needed a little time every Monday morning (which was his day off) to relax, write, read the paper and just enjoy some quiet time to himself. These precious hours replenished him and made a huge difference in how the rest of the week would go for both of us. As his wife, I recognized how important this was to him and really tried to make sure that he was able to do that.

   c. Every once in a while…

- A day to yourself.
  - Leisurely doing things that replenish you.
  - Pampering yourself.
  - No need to watch a clock or rush through a meal.
- A night away.
  - Short on cash? Have a sleepover at a friend's house and watch movies all night.
  - Get a hotel and have a romantic night with your husband.
  - Go to a retreat or conference where you'll be inspired and replenished.
- Take a vacation.

When you're fighting burnout, it's very important to...

4. Talk about it.

I will be honest with someone about everything. —*Hitting the Wall* by David Argue

a. Share what is going on with someone in your world.

b. Just opening up about your feelings, failures and frustrations can bring healing.

c. Isolating yourself will just add to the cycle of burnout.

d. Have safe people in your life who you know will hold you up and encourage you:

- husband
- prayer partner
- family Member
- friend
- small Group
- support Group

e. Don't be afraid to talk to a professional if you are facing significant struggles or your burnout doesn't seem to be getting better over time:

- christian Counselor
- pastor
- prayer Counseling Ministry
- mentor or Teacher
- doctor

Lesson Three

It's also very important to learn how to….

5. Simplify.

    a. You may *WANT* to be involved in five different small groups, but is it really the best thing for you in the long run?

    b. Do what you can and let that be enough.

- Everything doesn't have to be perfect.
- You don't have to do everything that everyone wants you to do.
- Learn how to say "NO."
- Lower your expectations for yourself and others.

    c. Prioritize.

- There is only so much energy you have every day. Learn to prioritize the things that are important to you and let the other things go.
- At the end of the day, what is REALLY valuable to you? Spend your energy on that.

    d. Single task orientation.

I know that as women we pride ourselves in being able to multi-task. We make dinner while we help with homework, while we text our boss, while we sort the laundry. But trying to do too much at one time can sometimes just raise your stress level. We become impatient with ALL the tasks we are trying to do, and end up not doing anything well. Instead of trying to do a lot of things at once, try and give your focused attention to a task, complete it and then move on. You might not get as much done, but you may find the process more enjoyable for everyone.

Another way to combat burnout, is to….

6. Ask for help.

    a. Why is this so hard to do?!?

    b. We feel like a failure if we can't do it all ourselves.

There's a great story in Exodus 18 about Moses learning this very important principle. Moses has led the Israelites out of captivity in Egypt and now they are in the wilderness, on their way to the land God had promised them. His father-in-law, Jethro, comes to visit, and he notices something that concerns him: The people would line up in front of Moses to bring their complaints against each other (Sounds like a FUN job to me). Moses would sit there from morning until evening, mediating the disagreements and conflicts amongst the people. Verse 14 shows us Jethro's advice.

When Moses' father-in-law saw all that Moses was doing for the people, he said, "Why are you trying to do all this alone? The people have been standing here all day to get your help."

"This is not good!" his father-in-law exclaimed. "You're going to wear yourself out—and the people too. This job is too heavy a burden for you to handle all by yourself."

Exodus 18:14, 17

Jethro encourages Moses to continue his role as the spiritual leader of the people, but to appoint capable, honest men to serve as leaders for the people's everyday needs and complaints.

Exodus 18:23

These men will help you carry the load, making the task easier for you. If you follow this advice, and if God directs you to do so, then you will be able to endure the pressures, and all these people will go home in peace.

   c. We need to determine what jobs are just too big for us to do alone and ask for help.

   d. Ask God to give you wisdom as to who to ask for help:

- husband
- extended family
- friends
- community
- babysitter

   e. Recognize that they might not do things exactly the way you would, but that you need to let them help you anyway.

f. Explore why you have such a hard time letting people help you:

- pride
- control
- selfishness
- needing to be needed
- having your identity in the things you *DO*

g. These aren't very godly character traits anyway, so you might as well lay them down and let someone help you!

God intends for us to know when we're hungry, lonely, in trouble, overwhelmed or in need of a break – and then take initiative to get what we need.
—*Boundaries* by Dr. Henry Cloud and Dr. John Townsend

And lastly, the most vital thing to healing is to….

7. Let Jesus lead you out of burnout.

a. He knows exactly what you need to replenish your body, mind and soul.

b. Trust Him to guide you through it.

- When He tells you to do something, *DO* it.
- When He tells you to *NOT* do something, *DON'T* do it.

c. Allow Him to replenish you.

- By His Word.
  - Write out scriptures that inspire you on note cards and put them around your house, car and in your purse to remind you of His promises.
  - Faithfully read the Bible and let it speak to you.
  - Find a church or teacher that feeds your soul and attend services, listen to podcasts or watch videos of their teaching.
- By His people.

- By friends lifting you up in prayer.

- By the encouragement that can be found in the Body of Christ.

- By surrounding yourself with people who challenge you in your walk of faith.

• By His Holy Spirit.

And I will ask the Father, and He will give you another Comforter (Counselor, Helper, Intercessor, Advocate, Strengthener and Standby), that He may remain with you forever.

John 14:16
AMP

- The Holy Spirit brings us comfort, strength, help and strength.

- He is the still, small voice in our hearts that whispers, "it's going to be okay."

- He will help us know what to do and give us the power and strength to do what He asks of us.

• By His direction.

- God will gently guide you as to the steps you should take to get back on track.

- He will lead you and speak wisdom into your heart as you determine to manage your life better.

• By His presence.

- There is no better place to find comfort than in the sweet presence of God.

- Spending time worshipping at His feet.

- Resting in His presence is *SO* healing.

- There is something supernatural that happens when we simply wait upon Jesus and let Him minister strength to our hearts, bodies and minds.

Lesson Three

> *We were crushed and completely overwhelmed, and we thought we would never live through it. But as a result, we learned not to rely on ourselves, but on God who can raise the dead. And he did deliver us from mortal danger. And we are confident that he will continue to deliver us.* –2 Corinthians 1:8

GROUP DISCUSSION QUESTIONS:

Some of the symptoms of burnout that we discussed today were:

- fatigue
- apathy
- irritability
- temper outbursts
- self-criticism
- cynicism
- negativity
- feeling besieged
- feeling overwhelmed
- helplessness

Discuss which of these symptoms are making an appearance in your home lately. ☺ What are some ways you could simplify your days? And don't say, "I can't," there's always *SOMETHING* that we could let go of to make our lives easier. ☺

- Why do you think it is so hard for us to ask for help when we need it?

GOING DEEPER

Here is one source's definition of burnout:

Burnout is a state of emotional, mental and physical exhaustion caused by excessive and prolonged stress. It occurs when you feel overwhelmed and unable to meet constant demands. As the stress continues, you begin to lose the interest or motivation that led you to take on a certain role in the first place. (helpguide.org)

Think back on your life. Has there been a season where you were experiencing these symptoms? **Describe the circumstances surrounding this time of your life.**

Is burnout something you are dealing with right now? **List the physical and emotional signs you are experiencing.**

The space below is provided for you to do an honest evaluation of your life and circumstances. **Be honest and give careful thought to each area.**

- Look at all the areas of your life and make an honest assessment of your health in these areas.

  - Your relationships

  - Your health (diet, exercise, rest, controlling health issues)

  - Your spiritual health

-   Your work situation

-   Your pace and level of activity

-   Your expectations

- What is causing you stress and anxiety?

- What do you need to accept that you cannot change and let go of?

- What can you change?

- List three things that you are committing to change in the next week.

List two ways you can take a break:

Everyday:

Every week:

Every once in awhile:

Who can you open up to about your struggles? If you're not being open with some-one now, think of a person who you can connect with and trust with your feelings.

What are some ways you can simplify your life? What are some expectations you can lay down? How can you prioritize the things in your life to get the best of your energy and attention?

Is there an area of your life that you need to ask someone for help? What is it and who do you think could help you?

Spend a few minutes praying and sitting in God's presence. What wisdom and direction is He giving you as to how to manage your life better? **Listen to His voice and write out anything you feel Him say to you.**

Psalm
63:1-8
NIV

O God, you are my God, earnestly I seek you; my soul thirsts for you, my body longs for you, in a dry and weary land where there is no water. I have seen you in the sanctuary and beheld your power and your glory.

Because your love is better than life, my lips will glorify you. I will praise you as long as I live, and in your name I will lift up my hands. My soul will be satisfied as with the richest of foods; with singing lips my mouth will praise you.

On my bed I remember you; I think of you through the watches of the night. Because you are my help, I sing in the shadow of your wings. My soul clings to you; your right hand upholds me.

The Weight of the World

SURVIVING GUILT

Guilt: The gift that keeps on giving. —Erma Bombeck

Morning. The sun peeks through the sheer waves in my curtain panels and I open my eyes to realize that yet again, a new day has arrived. I take a deep breath in, stretch my arms up and a smile appears on my lips.

And then I remember…

Suddenly the list of things that I need to do that day begins to file through my mind. It goes something like this:

"Don't forget that Lucy needs field trip money and Charlie needs a note because you have to pick him up early from school and take him to the dentist; and Betty has a birthday party on Friday so you need to pick up a present that doesn't cost more than $10 because this month the bills are a little tight; which reminds me that I need to go online and check out that new site that helps you get good deals at the grocery store; and while I'm there I need to order some flowers for my friend whose dog just died … except that is going to cost more money… so maybe I can just stop by her house and give her a hug in-between the volunteer meeting at church and taking a meal to my grandpa; and don't forget to get the last two chapters of my Bible Study finished and sent to the editor before five o'clock when Jeff gets home … which reminds me that he was out of clean socks, so I need to make sure I get the laundry finished … oh yeah, the washing machine is on the fritz so I need to call the repair man … shoot … more money … maybe I can look it up online and fix it myself in-between Dottie's nap and picking Betty up from kindergarten."

At this point, I feel the knot in my stomach rising and all I want to do is pull the covers over my head and go back to sleep.

The amount of things that are piled on our plates each and every day can be totally overwhelming. Not to mention the things going on in our minds….

I would say that I feel guilty most of the time. Guilty for not being a better wife, mom, daughter, granddaughter and sister. Guilty for not keeping my house cleaner. Guilty for not calling my friends more often. Guilty for not doing more at church. Guilty for not sending a note to that family having a hard time. Guilty for not volunteering in my kids' classrooms.

Why do we feel guilty all the time?

1. The *perception* of perfection.

    a. Everybody looks perfect from the outside. ☺

- We think other people's marriages are better.
- We think other people's houses are cleaner (which, in my case, is MOST DEFINITLY TRUE!).
- We think other people's jobs are more glamorous and rewarding.
- We think other people's kids are better behaved.

    b. We compare ourselves to our *PERCEPTION* of how other people's lives look and put unrealistic expectations on yourselves and our families.

- The truth is that *NOBODY'S* perfect … even if they look really good from the outside.
- When you are trying to live up to a standard of what you *THINK* other people are living up to, you are going to be constantly disappointed.

    c. We compare ourselves to the *PERCEPTION* we find in the media about the way we "should" do things.

In a day and age when you can find complete books on the proper way to launder your sheets, unending articles on how to parent your children the "correct" way and relentless pressure to do what everyone else is doing, we can easily get caught in the trap that we are not measuring up. We think we should be able to do everything perfectly all the time. The expectations that we put on ourselves to be "every woman" can set us up for much disappointment and failure.

- Trying to do everything the "right" way is exhausting.
- Trying to make your house look like the homes you see on TV is unrealistic.
- Trying to follow the advice on every article in every parenting technique is impossible.

- Sometimes we are overwhelmed with so many resources, and instead of helping and inspiring us, they simply confirm our fears that we're just not doing a good job.

d. We struggle with the idea of:

- "This is what a *GOOD* wife does...."
- "This is what a *GOOD* mother does...."
- "This is what a *GOOD* Christian does...."
- "This is what a *GOOD* business woman does...."

Another reason we struggle with guilt is....

2. We have a "god complex."

a. A "god complex" is a term used to describe someone who thinks they can do more than humanly possible.

b. We think that we can "do it all."

c. Often times we think that we can do it better than anyone else, so *OF COURSE* we should be the one to do it.

d. We think, "If I don't do it, it won't get done."

e. We see so much need around us and we don't stop to ask ourselves if we are really the best person to handle it ... we simply do it ourselves.

Oh my goodness, I am *so* guilty of this! *SOMEONE* needs to take a meal to the lady who just had surgery ... so of course it should be me. *SOMEONE* needs to make sure the kids' department has new crafts for Sunday School ... so of course I should make them. *SOMEONE* needs to make sure that the kindergarten class has all the hearts properly cut out for the Valentine's Day Party ... so of course I should cut them all out. I am guilty of thinking that I'm the only one who can handle these things, and if I don't handle them, I am riddled with guilt.

We also struggle with guilt because....

3. We want to make everyone happy.

a. Many of us struggle with "people-pleasing" issues.

- We don't want people to be disappointed in us.
- We don't want to say no to anyone.

Lesson Four

- We are more worried about what other people think about us than truly living the life God has called us to live.

b. We can't stand the idea of someone being upset with us.

c. We turn into people who have the "fear of man" instead of the "fear of God."

If I were still trying to please men, I would not be Christ's servant.
– Galatians 1:10

Another reason we struggle with guilt is….

4. We need to be needed.

a. Our identity is wrapped up in the things we are doing for other people.

b. We only feel valued when someone needs us.

c. THEY become our source of security, self-worth and value.

d. When we're not needed, we feel like we are nothing.

e. Unfortunately, this habit taints our relationships because we end up depending on other people to make us feel good, and therefore we are using them instead of actually serving them.

Our problem is that we NEED them (for ourselves) more than we LOVE them (for the glory of God.) The task God sets for us is to need them less, and love them more.

When People are Big and God is Small by Ed Welch

Some of you are struggling with guilt because....

5. You're trying to do it all ... but you're doing it alone.

    a. Maybe you don't have a strong support system around you.

    b. Maybe you're a single mom.

    c. Maybe your spouse's work schedule causes you to be by yourself a lot.

    d. Maybe your spouse doesn't share responsibilities.

    e. Trying to keep up with all of your responsibilities, without help from other people, can leave you feeling discouraged and guilty that you are not getting it all done.

"This is not who I am. I can be fun too, when I'm not solely responsible for holding everything together, nagging and taking care of the family.

> *The DNA of Relationships for Couples* by Dr. Greg Smalley & Dr. Robert S. Paul

The last reason we feel so guilty is....

6. We're so overcommitted, we can't POSSIBLY keep up with our schedules and the byproduct is: GUILT. We have:

    a. Packed schedules

    b. Overbooked commitments

    c. Out of control obligations

We are setting ourselves up for failure over and over again.

When we are unable to do what is before us with gentleness and kindness, we have lost sight of our calling and are sporting more hats than heart.

—*I Love Being a Woman* by Patsy Clairmont

Lesson Four

How can we get ditch the guilt?

1. Pitch the perfection.

    a. Stop comparing yourself to others.

- God did not make you like everyone else.

- You are going to have your *OWN* way of doing things.

- You don't need to pile on the guilt because you don't do things the way other people do them.

- Determine to live *YOUR* life the best way YOU know how.

- Remember that no one is perfect … even if they look like it from the outside.

    b. Do your best to honor God in every area of your life and let that be enough.

- Faithfully be the best wife, mother, daughter, friend, employee that you can be; and let that be enough.

- Trust God to help you grow in these areas, and let honoring Him be your motivation … not simply trying to avoid guilt.

And whatever you do or say, do it as a representative of the Lord Jesus, giving thanks through him to God the Father. –Colossians 3:17

    c. Relax.

- Is it *REALLY* the end of the world if your house stays messy another day?

- Is it *REALLY* worth getting so stressed out if things don't go exactly as you had planned?

- Is it *REALLY* important enough to become nagging, frustrated and no fun to be around?!

- Life is short; let the small stuff stay small.

    d. Be realistic.

- You may *WANT* to have your house decorated like a showroom, but your budget and the ages of the residents in your home just might make that impossible.

- Set yourself up to succeed. You may have to put some things on the shelf for a few weeks, months or even years until your life and circumstances are different.

My grandmother was an incredible seamstress, and she always sewed clothes, curtains and pillows--and even dolls and toys for her family. When my kids were little, I remember her saying to me, "You know, when my kids were young, I just packed up my sewing machine and put it away. I took it out again when they were three. It just wasn't worth the frustration to try and sew when my kids needed so much energy and time from me." I always remembered that advice, and have tried to simply embrace the season of life that I'm in instead of trying to FIGHT it. I learned to accept that some things are just harder to do in a certain stage of life and if I'm just patient, that season will come around again in time.

Another way to get past guilt is to....

2. Be honest about your limits.

    a. Unfortunately, you are *NOT* super woman. ☺

    b. When you commit to so many things that it's simply not possible to get them all done, guilt is an inevitable by-product.

    c. Be realistic about the hours in the day and the time you have.

    d. Realize that every time you say *YES* to something you are saying *NO* to something else.

    e. Be diligent about not over-extending yourself.

You also need to....

3. Recognize that you need to honor God with your life MORE than you need to make everyone else happy:

So they worshipped the things God made, but not the Creator himself....
–Romans 1:25

Lesson Four

Oh my, am I on a journey of learning not to be a "people pleaser." God has really been dealing with this issue in my heart. The bottom line is, when I am looking to make everyone else happy, I am "fearing man" more than I am "fearing God." In essence, people become my god. I want to do everything *THEY* say. I want to make sure *THEY* are happy; I look to *THEM* for approval, and if I disappoint them in any way, I can hardly stand it. I wish I could say that I am as diligent in making sure I do everything GOD says, and that I am as concerned that *HE* is pleased with me, and that I would be just as bothered at the thought of disobeying *HIM* or not honoring *HIM*, as I am with other people.

    a. Determine to live to please God and not man.

    b. Recognize the "people pleasing" mentality in you when it begins to rise up.

- When you're tempted to say "yes" to something you really don't want to do because you don't want to upset someone.

- When you say "no" to something because you're so fearful of what people might think of you.

- When criticism cripples you and the opinion someone else has of you easily becomes your opinion of yourself.

- When you don't speak up but instead let people take advantage of you.

    c. Live to please God alone.

> *The most radical treatment for the fear of man is the fear of the Lord. God must be bigger to you than people are.*
>
> —*When People are Big and God is Small* by Ed Welch

Another way you can ditch the guilt is to….

4. Learn how to do only the things God is asking you to do.

    a. It can be very hard to figure out what things you should do and what things you shouldn't do.

    b. We have to come to Jesus with our schedule, responsibilities and decisions.

    c. Learn not to commit to anything until you pray about it and ask God if it's something you should or should not do.

For this reason, since the day we heard about you, we have not stopped praying for you. We continually ask God to fill you with the knowledge of his will through all the wisdom and understanding that the Spirit gives, so that you may live a life worthy of the Lord and please him in every way; bearing fruit in every good work, growing in the knowledge of God, being strengthened with all power according to his glorious light so that you may have great endurance and patience.

> Colossians
> 1:9-11

    d. Ask God to give you the knowledge of His will so that you will only do the things that are going to bear good fruit.

    e. Be mindful of areas where you have allowed boundaries to be blurred.

    f. Determine to stay only within the boundaries of the things God has asked of you.

Another way to combat guilt is to....

5. Stop the needy cycle.

    a. Recognize that when you are doing things for other people because you need to be needed, you are using them.

    b. To truly love and serve people, you need to freely give without looking for them to fill you up.

I've learned that this is vital – even in my marriage. There are times that I catch myself getting annoyed at my husband when he doesn't seem to be "filling me up" the way I want him to. I get mad at him if he doesn't compliment me; I get frustrated if he doesn't notice something I've done for him. When I'm really honest, and get to the heart of the matter, I recognize that I am looking to Jeff to make me feel better about myself--a role he was *NEVER* meant to fill. Even if he did his very best every second of every day, he just was not created to know my every need and be able to fill it. I am *WAY* too needy … he would be exhausted!!!

I must go to Jesus for every single ounce of my self- worth. He alone knows my heart and what I need; He alone can speak value and significance to my heart. My identity *MUST* be found in Him alone.

Once I receive from God, then I am able to love my husband without needing anything in return. If he compliments me, it's awesome, but my value doesn't depend on it. If he does something nice for me, it's icing on the cake. I am already full in Christ, and therefore anything I do for Jeff is simply out of love and not a manipulation to try and get him to do the same in return.

c. Keep your heart full of Jesus – and let your giving be out of the abundance.

You also need to realize that....

6. Flying solo means flying differently.

a. If you find yourself in a season where you don't have people around you to help, and everything is riding on your shoulders alone, first of all … I am so sorry.

- Know that God sees you and although you might feel alone, you most definitely are *not* alone.
- My *FAVORITE* name of God is Emmanuel: God is with us. He is with you--always.
- And God will bring people into your life to come along side and support, encourage and help you.
- Begin praying for the arrival of those people and do not lose heart in the waiting.

b. If you are facing life alone, you have to look at things differently.

- You might have to simplify your life even more.
- You might need to look for help from other sources:
  - your church
  - other friends in similar situations
  - support groups and outreaches

c. Let people help you.

- I know it can be hard to accept help.
- You need it and people really do want to help you.

7. Let yourself off the hook.

The truth is, you probably will ALWAYS have a million things to do every day. But once you make an honest assessment of your life (which we will go into more deeply in the next chapter), get rid of the baggage that makes you commit to things you shouldn't commit to, and determine to live in God's plan for your today, then there's nothing left to do but just let it go. Do what you can do, and let that be enough: It's time to ditch the guilt.

> Come unto me, all you who are weary and burdened, and I will give you rest. Take my yoke upon you and learn from me, for I am gentle and humble in heart, and you will find rest for your souls. For my yoke is easy and my burden is light.
>
> Matthew 11:28-30

GROUP DISCUSSION QUESTIONS

- What are some of the areas of your life in which you struggle with guilt?

- What do you think are the underlying reasons for your guilt? Perfectionism? People pleasing? Needing to be needed? Over commitment?

- What is one thing that you could change in order to feel less pressure and guilt in your life?

Lesson Four

GOING DEEPER

When you lay your head down at night, or wake up first thing in the morning, how do you feel about the state of your life? Are you feeling content and satisfied? Or are you feeling overwhelmed and guilty that you aren't keeping up with everything?

We discussed the stress that the perception of perfection can have on us. What are some areas in which you struggle in wanting to have everything perfect?

How can you let go of some of those expectations? What is a realistic expectation for that area of life?

Is there an area of your life where you have a "god complex?" Are you trying to do more than humanly possible? List some ideas here as to how you can change this.

Do you struggle with "people pleasing?" What are you afraid will happen if you make someone unhappy? Where do you think this fear comes from?

Write out Jeremiah 17:5-7 here.

Do you find that you need to be needed? How do you feel when someone really needs your help? How do you feel when you are *NOT* needed?

In what ways do you think you can LOVE people more and NEED them less? Give a few examples.

Are you in a season of life where you are facing things alone? Are you holding on to resentment or bitterness because of your situation? If you are, <u>lay it down</u>. **Write out a prayer of forgiveness and ask God to bring someone alongside to help you.**

Are there areas of your life in which you realize you have not had adequate boundaries? What are those areas?

What practical steps do you need to take in order to have healthy boundaries?

This is My Life

OWNING IT AND LIVING IT

> *I believe you should live every day as if it is your last. Which is why I don't have any clean laundry, because, come one who wants to wash clothes on the last day of their life?* —Anonymous

One of my favorite little pastimes is imagining what my life will be like in 20 years. Just think ... when it's time to walk out the door, I just grab my purse and go. No diaper bags; no snacks and juice cups; no extra change of clothes for the "almost-potty-trained-but-still-not-potty-trained–enough-to-keep-from-peeing-in-the-middle–of-the–grocery- store" moments. I could just go to a movie on the spur of the moment – no baby-sitters needed. The only messes – are the ones I make ... and Jeff too, I guess. But he for sure will be neater in 20 years. The huge office that will have replaced the piles of toys in the spare room ... aaahhh.

I know that I'm supposed to embrace the season I'm in. I know that it goes so fast and if you blink, you'll miss it. I know all of these things; but knowing these things doesn't necessarily mean that it helps me on the days when I feel like I just can't keep my head above water.

And the ironic thing about this type of daydreaming, is that it's all really just an illusion anyway. I'm sure if I ask anyone of you in the "teenager" season of life, you would say that the diaper stuff was *EASY* compared to this!

And those of you with kids in college would argue that you would *MUCH* prefer to hire a babysitter for the evening--assured that your children are safe and sound, as opposed to dealing with your kids being outside of your watchful eye and praying they make good choices and right decisions.

And my mother, who is now spending the majority of her time caring for her aging and ailing parents, would say that this season of life is far more difficult than she had ever imagined.

And that's pretty much the way it goes for most of us, isn't it? The grass indeed is greener on the other side. Everything looks better when it's not what we are dealing with in the moment. And if we're not careful, we can dream our days away and find that our hearts are in a perpetual state of discontent.

My son has an *EXTREMELY* frustrating habit. If the television is on, he is absolutely transfixed by it; he can walk in the door and be completely at the other end of the house and instantly his mind is locked onto whatever is happening on the TV. I have watched in total amazement as he has tried to tie his shoes, do his homework and even eat his food, without the slightest glance away from the television. I literally could put brussel sprouts, fried liver and prunes on his plate and if the TV was on, I'm not quite sure he would even notice; when he's fixed on it, he cannot see anything else.

You and I can do the same thing: We fix our eyes on anything and everything, except the thing right in front of us, and we can become completely disengaged, ineffective and frustrated.

I truly believe that one of the greatest traps we can fall into is not "owning our lives." Instead of purposefully embracing our season and lot, we miss out because our eyes are firmly fixed somewhere else: our lives as they are right now seem unfortunate and we are no longer living our lives – we're looking forward to the mythical "better life."

What are some of the ways we don't "own our lives?"

1. "The Grass is Greener"

    a. We think that every other possible scenario of life is better than the one we are in.

    b. We think it will be better when:

- my kids are older
- I'm married
- we have more money
- I can go back to work
- I have more time

c. We are constantly discontent....

- We look at what is in our hands and it seems laborsome and menial.

- We become resentful of the things we have to do, because our hearts are fixed on something else.

d. We miss out on what is in front of us today....

- You cannot be focused on something ahead of you and be fully present where you are right now.

- When you are not fully engaged in your life, you don't do your very best.

- You're not growing, developing and learning the lessons you should be learning in this season.

Another way we don't "own our lives" is...

2. "Living on Autopilot"

There were 25 pounds left. I was desperately trying to lose the last of the baby weight that I had gained, and so I was searching for ways that I could cut back on my exceptional love for food. I suddenly realized that the greatest hindrance to my overeating was simply not being AWARE of what I was eating. Grabbing a handful of M&Ms because they were sitting right on the counter; mindlessly grabbing the last chicken nugget from my kids' Happy Meals without thinking about whether or not I was actually still hungry; fixing myself a bowl of ice cream before bed because I was just in the habit of doing it.

There are *COUNTLESS* ways that you and I walk through our daily lives on auto-pilot. Doing what we've always done: Not consciously making decisions and choices, but simply reacting and doing things without any thought or intention.

Oh! Teach us to live well! Teach us to live wisely and well! —Psalm 90:12 MSG

a. Going through the day without thinking.

- What you are going to do?

- Where you are going to spend your time?

- Who you are going to impact?

Lesson Five

- What God is asking you to do with *TODAY*?

b. Not making the most of our days, but just aimlessly getting through them.

c. Making decisions without praying and aligning them with your desires.

d. Not being fully "present."

- Having your face in your phone instead of engaging with your family.
- Having the TV on without noticing.
- Not connecting with the people you meet, but being inside your own head, in your own little bubble.

How often do you check out in a grocery store and not even notice the person working there? How often do you walk through a crowd of people without consciously looking at the people around you? How many afternoons do you breeze past your spouse or kids without listening to their stories about their day? We can become so disengaged with what is going on around us; people become a means to an end for us and we fail to SEE the people in our world.

- We make no time for reflection.

Another way we don't "own our lives" is....

3. Following the "Status Quo"

a. We do it because "that's the way it's done."

b. We look at how outside influences (the media and culture) say our lives should look.

- Dictating our consumerism and lifestyle.
- Activities in which our kids are involved.
- The size and appearance of our houses.
- Our income.
- Where we spend our time and energy.
- How we spend our money.

c. We make decisions based on maintaining a certain lifestyle:

- Our desire to be comfortable and secure outweighs our desire to be fulfilled and purposeful.

- We find ourselves caught in the trap of maintaining what we've achieved and accumulated – even if we find that it's not what we're really passionate about any more.

So often I feel like I am spinning in the little hamster wheel of the suburban life: Don't think, Kristie, just sign 'em up and write a check; don't ask questions, just get in the car and go; don't make things more complicated, just get through the day and then go to bed. I am not living my life; my life is <u>living me</u>.

And the last way in which we don't "own our lives"….

4. We simply "Check Out."

We all have seen it time and time again. The friend. The neighbor. The girl from your small group. You notice a sense of disengagement. You see them withdraw and pull back. They have lost the light in their eyes and even though they are there, they are not really *THERE*. Why? Because they are unhappy. Their lives are not going well. The don't like their husband very much anymore. Their kids are struggling and they are weary of trying to help them. They've been hurt by the church. They've lost a sense of purpose and direction. Whatever the reason may be, there is something that happens when you are unhappy, and you feel powerless to do anything about it.

   a. We stop looking forward because we do not envision the future to be very bright.

   b. We withdraw because we are tired of looking for the positive in the situation.

   c. We feel trapped: We've tried to make changes, but it seems that nothing ever helps.

   d. Going through the motions seems to be the only way to make it through the day.

   e. Accepting that this just may "be the way it is" is our only coping mechanism.

Peace has been stripped away, and I have forgotten what prosperity is. I cry out, "My splendor is gone. Everything I had hoped for from the Lord is lost."

Lamentations
3:17-18

Lesson Five

So, how can we take ownership of our lives and be fully present?

1. Embrace your season.

> *There is a time for everything, a season for every activity under heaven.*
> —Ecclesiastes 3:1

    a. Determine to live in *THIS* moment, in *THIS* life, at THIS time with all that comes with it … the good, the bad and the ugly.

    b. Instead of focusing on what lies ahead of you, focus on how you can make *THIS* moment the very best it can be.

> *And don't be wishing you were someplace else or with someone else. Where you are right now is God's place for you. Live and obey and love and believe right there.*
> 1 Corinthians 7:17 MSG

- Spend some time looking at the *BENEFITS* that this season of life affords you

I remember a few years ago when it seemed like all I ever did was drive my kids around. Between half-day kindergarten, preschool, private therapy, music lessons and carpool, I found myself *ALWAYS* in my car. I was getting very frustrated because I felt like I coul never get anything done: There wasn't enough time in-between all of my appointments to do anything significant (like grocery shopping or anything remotely fun!), but yet the collective time I spent waiting around caused me to feel like I was not very productive at all.

This was all exacerbated because the previous season of life in which I was hunkered down with little babies in the house afforded me A LOT of time to write and study. While the kids napped, I would sneak away and work on a lesson for the Bible Study I was teaching at the time. I was able to stay in my jammies all day long and simply linger between loving on my babies (which was *HEAVEN*) and doing the thing I loved most, which was writing. I *LOVED* the pace of life during those years.

And *NOW!* Always running. Always late. Always stressed. This new season and I were *NOT* friends.

I was full-on whining about this to Jesus one day, when I clearly heard Him say, "If you'd stop complaining about this, and look at it from a different perspective, you might be able to see the benefits of this time of your life instead of only seeing the negative."

So, I decided to get creative. I packed a little bag to keep in my car with a Bible, journal, some books I had been wanting to read for a long time and a highlighter. Whenever I dropped the kids off, I would pull out my bag and begin studying. It was surprising how many "God moments" I had in my mini-van during those years. It truly became "holy ground" for me and I began to look forward to those times when God would meet me in my car.

   c. Think about some of the distinctive things about this time in your life that you will never get to experience again.

   • Maybe you are in a season of "singleness" and you are struggling with loneliness.

      - Before I was married, I remember saying to God, "I just have so much love in me that I want to give to someone." And God spoke to me, "There are SO many people who don't have *ANYONE* to love them. How about finding some of them and giving them your love?"

      - Find a way to use the advantages of your singleness!

I want you to live as free of complications as possible. When you're unmarried, you're free to concentrate on simply pleasing the Master. Marriage involves you in all the nuts and bolts of domestic life and in wanting to please your spouse, leading to so many more demands on your attention. The time and energy that married people spend on caring for and nurturing each other, the unmarried can spend in becoming whole and holy instruments of God. I'm trying to be helpful and make it as easy as possible for you, not make things harder. All I want is for you to be able to develop a way of life in which you can spend plenty of time together with the Master without a lot of distractions.

1 Corinthians
7:32-35
MSG

Lesson Five

- Think about the relationships you can develop in this season of life.
    - Maybe you're in a season where your kids are involved in lots of sports. Take advantage of the time you have sitting with other moms twice a week and reach out to someone new.
    - Maybe you're working full time in a job you're not crazy about – but it's paying the bills. Take this season to be a light in the workplace. Consider the amazing opportunity to share the love of Jesus with your co-workers.
    - Maybe you're going through something scary with your health. Perhaps you can be an encouragement to others around you going through the same thing.
    - Maybe you are going through a season where life has significantly slowed down and you are missing the fast pace and achievement you used to have. Take this time to wait on God; grow closer to Him while you have more quiet space.
- Focusing on the uniqueness of this time of life will help you appreciate its value.

d. If you're always looking ahead, you'll miss what's right in front of you.

Sacred Rhythms by Ruth Hayley Barton

Something inside me stood at attention and said, this is my life. This is what it's like to be all the way here now rather than always longing for something else. This is my life as it is meant to be lived in God.

e. Remember that every season has its challenges and rewards.

f. Trust the timing.
- God's plan for you *RIGHT NOW* will *FIT* into your season of life.
- Frustration will come when we try to do something God HASN'T called us to right now, and we can't seem to make it work.

You have just enough time to do God's will. If you can't get it all done, it means you are trying to do more than God intended for you to do.

—*The Purpose Driven Life* by Rick Warren

- Recognize that sometimes God has given you a dream to be realized in the future, but you must be faithful in your current season because it's a season of preparation.

Well done, my good and faithful servant. You have been faithful in handling this small amount, so now I will give you many more responsibilities.

Matthew 25:21

Another way you can "own your life" is to....

1. Be fully engaged in your daily life.

a. Be conscious about decisions.
- Where should I be spending my time today?
- Where should I be spending my energy?
- Who should I be purposefully engage with today?
- How can I order my day to bring the most glory to God?

Don't live carelessly, unthinkingly. Make sure you understand what the Master wants. —Ephesians 5:17 MSG

Lesson Five

b. Be conscious of every moment, not mindlessly walking through your day.

- Ask God to guide your every step and word.
  - What do you want me to do now?
  - What do you want me to say to this person?
  - How do you want me to handle this conflict?
  - What should I spend my time focusing on for today?

c. Be fully present with the people in your world:

- turn off the TV
- turn off the computer
- put your phone away
- give them undivided attention
- listen
- ask questions
- pay attention
- be thoughtful
- notice
- compliment
- speak up

d. Make time for reflection and prayer throughout your day.

- Start your morning by reading the Bible and asking God to give you direction for your day.
- Take moments throughout your day to pray for people and situations as the Holy Spirit brings them to mind.
- Take the time to repent of wrong attitudes, sinful behaviors and places where you fell short.
- Ask God to give you the words to say when you face decisions.
- At the end of the day, reflect on what God has done and give thanks for all of His blessings.

Another way you can "own your life" is to….

2. Have the courage to live the life God has designed for *YOU* alone.

a. Avoid the temptation to do things "the way everyone else is doing them" or "the way they've always been done."

b. Figure out what God's plan is for you.

c. Don't be afraid to be different and take risks for God.

This has been a very personal journey for Jeff and me. A few years ago, we felt that God was calling us to a new season of life and ministry. We had been music pastors for fifteen years, and were very happy doing "what we had always done," but we felt God stirring something new inside both of us. After a couple of years praying about that stirring, the moment came where we felt God tell us it was time.

Time for what? That is a very good question.

He didn't tell us that; the only thing we knew for sure was that Jeff was supposed to resign his position at church.

We both had many, many conversations with God, asking Him to give us more insight and direction. But He very clearly spoke to both of our hearts that we were to take a step, and *THEN* He would show us the way to go.

We wrestled with God on this for awhile, and I was surprised at the core of my struggles. I realized that I wondered if people would think we were crazy for quitting a job without knowing what we were going to do next. I worried that we wouldn't still be able to live in our nice house in our nice suburban neighborhood and buy nice things for our children. (Like … you know … FOOD!)

I was disappointed in myself when I finally realized my true fears. I was comfortable, very comfortable: I loved my church; I loved my house; I loved the stability and predictability of my life. But was that really what my life was supposed to be about?

Comfort sneaks up on you. I *THOUGHT* I was living a life of faith until God asked me to do something that made me *UNCOMFORTABLE*. To do something that didn't give me any guarantees other than *HE* would always take care of us. And why wouldn't that be enough for me? If He said He was going to guide us and provide for our needs, shouldn't that be all I needed?

Lesson Five

We realized that this was a much-needed lesson in our lives: We could either be safe and comfortable, living the life we had always lived and doing what was predictable … or we could take a step of faith and live the adventure that God had for us.

So we did it: We took the leap. We were like Abraham when God told him to leave without telling him where he was going. We quit our job and started this new season of life and ministry.

We still don't know exactly what our next steps are, but not for one second have we regretted taking the step. It has unlocked a season of faith in us that we have never experienced before. It has challenged the level of doubt and unbelief that was in our hearts. It has been amazing to watch Him provide for us, open doors for us and do miraculous things in our family.

We have a new motto: Life is short; God is *big*. We don't want to miss out on what He has for us because we are afraid to follow wherever He leads us.

    d. Make family decisions based on what's best for your family.

- Fight the temptation just to do what everyone else is doing.

- Be purposeful about the things in which you choose to be involved.

- Even if other people are pressuring you to do something, have the courage to do what is right for *YOU*.

People who own their lives do not feel guilty when they make choices about where they are going. They take other people into consideration, but when they make choices for the wishes of others, they are choosing out of love, not guilt; to advance a good, not to avoid being bad.

Boundaries by Dr. Henry Cloud and Dr. John Townsend

When taking ownership of your life, it's vitally important to....

3. Bring your unhappiness to Jesus.

  a. Don't check out on your life.

  b. God has *SO* much for you and desires to help you get to the other side of this season.

I have come to realize that when I find myself withdrawing from life and especially withdrawing from God, something significant has happened in my heart. On the surface it may look like I'm just frustrated with the circumstance, but in truth, the heart of the matter is this: I am doubting God's goodness. I feel like nothing is ever going to change and I am going to be stuck in this mess forever; I doubt that He is working; I doubt that He is going to intervene; I don't trust His way and His timing.

I believe that the enemy of our souls tries to manipulate us by taking our situation and trying to convince us that God doesn't care. When we are convinced that God doesn't care, we then feel justified to take matters into our own hands and try to fix it ourselves. And when that doesn't work, we simply begin to despair.

God cares *deeply* about your <u>life</u>. God cares deeply about your heart. God cares deeply about the <u>people in your world</u>. He doesn't want you to give up: He wants you to stay engaged with Him and with your life so that He can lead you through this season.

  c. Pour out your heart to God.

  • He is *NOT* afraid of your questions.

  • Engage with Him!

  • Tell Him what you are struggling with.

  • Continue to cry out to Him and ask Him to comfort you, guide you and speak to you.

  d. Stay in the Word.

  • Read through the Psalms--many of them are cries to God for help to get through difficult times.

  • Ask God to give you promises to hold on to.

  • Write out those promises and refer back to them in the moments when you feel discouraged.

Lesson Five

e. Remember the kindness of the Lord.

- Trust that His very character is *LOVE*.
- Trust that He will *NEVER* let you go.
- Trust that He is *ALWAYS* working on your behalf.
- Wait for Him: Do not get impatient; *trust* His timing.

> *Then I called on the name of the Lord: "Please save me!" How kind the Lord is! How good he is! So merciful, this God of ours!* –Psalm 116:4-5

f. What do you do in an unhappy marriage?

- Don't give up!
- Don't fall into temptation.
- Don't despair.
- Know that God is able to make *ALL* things new.
- Continually ask Him to heal your marriage and to change you both into the people He wants you to be.
- Determine to take whatever steps of obedience God asks you to take – even if you don't feel like it.

My dear, dear friends Joe and Jen Anderson went through an extraordinary struggle in their marriage. Fighting depression and addiction, they eventually separated for almost three years. God did an amazing work in each of them individually, and they determined that God was asking them to work on their marriage. Jen says, "We did it strictly out of obedience. When we moved back in together, we didn't love each other. We didn't even *LIKE* each other. But we knew that this was what God was asking of us." Over time God healed and restored their relationship and now they have an amazingly strong, vital marriage and have a ministry sharing their story to help others realize God can restore things that seem "un-restorable." (You can hear more about Joe and Jen's testimony and book them to speak to your church or group at surrenderstory.org)

g. What do you do when your children are struggling, and you're losing hope?

- Pray, pray, pray.
- Trust that God is with them and He *WILL* continue to draw them close to Him – even if you may not be able to see it right now.
- Continually place them back in the hands of God.
- Do not let your heart grow cold towards God because He isn't working the way you think He should.

h. What do you do if you've been hurt and can't seem to move forward?

- Forgive those who have hurt you.
- Trust God for your healing.
- Don't get stuck in bitterness.
- Keep your eyes on Jesus and not other people.

i. What do you do if you've lost your purpose?

- Ask God for a new vision.
- Resist the lie that "your best days are behind you."
- Realize that God has things for you <u>now</u>!
- Take steps toward something--if you refuse to move out of fear or uncertainty, you'll never get anywhere.

"For I know the plans I have for you," says the Lord. "They are plans for good and not for disaster, to give you a future and a hope." –Jeremiah 29:11

Lesson Five

4. Live a God-centered life.

Many of us wonder how to balance all of our roles. I've tried making lists: God is first, Jeff is second, my kids are third, my job is fourth ... but that never seems to work. What about the days when my job needs a lot of my attention? Then I spend the day feeling somehow like I have my priorities messed up. But God has called me to be a good steward at my job as well as being a good parent to my kids, right? And what about the days the kids need me more?

It's true that we need to keep our faith and family first. But within the framework of our lives, how are we to know if we are giving the time and energy needed to each and every part?

I have learned that there is only one way to do this: It's by living a "God-centered life."

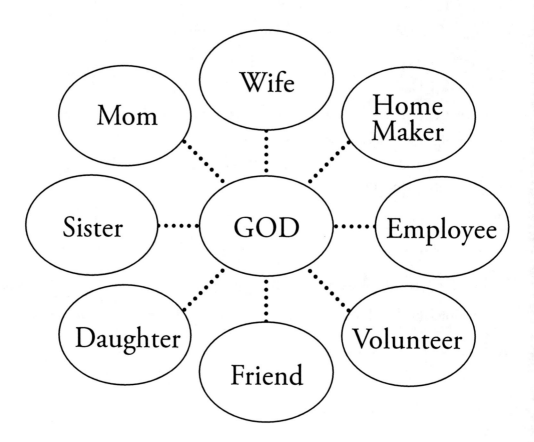

a. What that means is, **the most important thing is our relationship with God.**

- We keep Him at the center.
- We make sure we spend time with Him every day.
- We keep our hearts pure – letting Him correct wrong attitudes or areas that are out of balance.
- We are listening for His direction and guidance.

b. Then everything else flows out of our relationship with God.

- We ask Him to guide us.
- We ask Him to give us instruction, insight and wisdom as to how to fulfill all of those roles.

c. Then our priorities simply become this: **Do whatever God tells you to do.**

- Let the Holy Spirit order your life, whispering wisdom as to how to be the best at all the things you need to be.
- There will be seasons when He speaks to your heart to focus less on your career, and more on your husband.
- There will be seasons when He speaks to you about focusing less on your house, and more on your friends.
- Ask God to give you goals and direction for each specific area and insight as to how to best serve in each of the roles you fill.

d. Not only will He give you big picture wisdom, He will give you everyday guidance as well.

- Discernment to spend a little more time with your teenager today because He knows that they need it.
- Wisdom to spend a little less time on the computer because you need to get caught up on your responsibilities at home.
- Direction to make time in your day for some quiet time with your spouse because you need some connection and communication.
- Instruction to lay aside one area of ministry in order to enter a different area of service.

Lesson Five

e. God is concerned about how you spend your days. Ask Him:
  - "God, how can I be the mother you want me to be today?"
  - "God, how can I be the wife you want me to be today?"
  - "God, how can I be the homemaker you want me to be today?"
  - "God, how can I serve my church and community today?"
  - "God, how can I be the daughter and sister you want me to be today?"
  - "God, how can I be the friend you want me to be today?"
  - "God, how can I be the employee you want me to be today?

f. When God is ordering your day, there will always be enough time to get everything done.
  - He will help guide your schedule and help you to not over commit.
  - But I also believe with *ALL MY HEART*, that when we submit our responsibilities and schedules to Him, He *SUPERNATURALLY* gives us the ability to do more and be more effective.

There have been seasons of life that we lived at a crazy pace—but those were seasons where we knew we were simply doing what God had placed in front of us to do. And although I remember being very tired, I also remember a supernatural infusion of grace and energy, a protection for my marriage and children, and insight and direction that I knew could come only from God.

I am confident that it was God's supernatural power working in and through me. If you added it all up, it really shouldn't make sense. But that's God. When we allow Him to have the reins, He will use you in ways you never thought imaginable or possible.

But seek first His Kingdom and His righteousness, and all these things will be given to you as well. —Matthew 6:33 NIV

Let's Get Practical:

Living a God-centered life requires you to ask *HIM* how He wants you to order your life. I typically do this once a year, but you might feel led to do it more or less than that. Here are a few of the things He has given me personally:

What have you called me to do right now?

- Slow down. (God specifically told me to "Do more by doing less.)
- Support and pray for direction for my husband.
- Be more present with my children – not always multi-tasking.
- Write and speak to women to encourage and disciple them.
- Spend time working on my home: specifically decorating areas that I've been meaning to decorate and going through clutter and closets.
- Encourage and draw out the ministry gifts of those around me.
- Support the Body of Christ by serving churches.
- Develop more meaningful relationships with my neighbors.

Some ways I can "walk this out:"

- Be mindful of over-committing and only take on projects I feel like God is telling me to take.
- Set aside time daily to pray for Jeff, and be sensitive to ways I can support and encourage him. (Specifically, reassuring his leadership of our family and making sure he knows "I'm with him.")
- Spend individual time with my children; learn to be a better listener to them.
- Be diligent about writing projects and faithfully follow the leading of the Holy Spirit as to that on which I should be working.
- Paint the bathroom!!!
- Make time for coffee with friends and people God brings into my path to encourage.
- Continue to ask God to direct my service in the church.
- Invite some neighbors over for lunch!

After I do this general list, I take some time and pray over every person and area of responsibility in my life. I ask God to give me three goals for each area.

MY LIFE LIST:

List each responsibility and three goals.

<u>My Spiritual Life and Health</u>

Jeff

Lucy

Charlie

Betty

Dottie

My Home

Work

Church

My Friends

My Extended Family

My Community

Teach us to make the most of our time, so that we may grow in wisdom.

–Psalm 90:12

GROUP DISCUSSION QUESTIONS

- What are some ways that you struggle to "own your life?" Are you tempted with "The Grass is Greener?" Or maybe it's living on "Autopilot?" Or perhaps you struggle with the "Status Quo" or simply "Checking Out?" Share some of your experiences with the group.

- What are some ways that you can begin to "own your life?" How can you be more engaged and purposeful about the season you are in?

- We talked about living a "God-Centered Life." Has God ever spoken specific direction for you in an area of your life? Share your story with the group.

GOING DEEPER

There are many ways in which we cannot fully be engaged and owning our lives.

Name some areas in which you've been tempted to think that "the grass is greener." How have you been tempted to miss out on the season you're in?

Name some of the benefits of the season of life you are now in. **Focus on the things that you will not experience during any other time in your life.**

Many of us live on "Autopilot." What are some things that you have done mindlessly – without being purposeful about your decisions and the way you are spending your time and energy.

Think of some ways you can be mindful of your decisions. List a few of them here.

What are some ways in which you are tempted to simply live "the Status Quo?"

What are some things that God is calling you to, yet you have been held back by your fear of the unknown or different? Or maybe you haven't even entertained the thought of doing something adventurous or different for awhile! Spend some time dreaming and thinking *BIG*. What would you love to do? **What kind of adventure could you and God have together?**

Perhaps you have been disengaged from your life because you are simply frustrated and unhappy. Take a moment and lay your soul bare before the Lord: **Write out your heart's honest questions and frustrations. He can handle it.**

Now ask God to give you insight, wisdom and some promises to get through this season and restore joy to your soul. **Write these promises here.**

Now it's YOUR turn to get practical!

Ask God: What have you called me to do right now?

Lesson Five

List some practical ways in which you can "walk this out:"

My Life List:

List each responsibility and three goals:

-

    –

    –

    –

-

    –

    –

    –

-

    –

    –

    –

-

  -
  -
  -

-

  -
  -
  -

-

  -
  -
  -

-

  -
  -
  -

-

  -
  -
  -

-

  -
  -
  -

-

  -
  -
  -

Lesson Five

Keep on asking, and you will be given what you ask for. Keep on looking, and you will find. Keep on knocking, and the door will be opened. For everyone who asks, receives. Everyone who seeks, finds. And the door is opened to everyone who knocks.

Matthew
7:7-8

Money, Money, Money

NOT LETTING MONEY RULE YOUR LIFE

Until you make peace with who you are, you'll never be content with what you have. —Doris Mortman

Someone stole all my credit cards, but I won't be reporting it. The thief spends less than my wife did. —Henny Youngman

Money, huh? Is that what you're asking yourself right now? A chapter on money? Right here in the middle of my Bible study about identity?

Yup. Here it is.

I thought it was a little strange too. But as I was studying and praying about the topics that should be included in this little book, the Holy Spirit continually brought me back to this topic.

Why?

As I have been on my own personal journey of finding my identity in Christ, this was something that kept rising to the surface in my heart. Money, and the role that it played in my life, was definitely something I needed to look at. When I'm really, really honest, a whole lot of my identity (or lack thereof) is directly linked to the things I'm buying (or not buying … or wishing I was buying … or pouting about because I am not buying … you get the picture.)

Contentment, greed, generosity, stewardship. These things are so tied into the framework of what makes up the ins and outs of our lives, that we would be naïve to think that money doesn't affect us on every, single level.

My point is this: There are very few things that can alter our mood, outlook or perspective, than money. I am easily swayed by its power; I am forever burdened by its weight. There isn't an area of my world that isn't directly related to the money in my bank account.

Like success, money is an emotionally volatile issue for most women. It's probably the most complicated relationship we have—and the one that most controls our lives because we let it.

Simple Abundance by Sara Ban Breathnach

Here are a few facts about money:

- Total U.S. revolving debt (98 percent of which is made up of credit card debt) $796.5 billion, as of November 2010 (Source: Federal Reserve's G.19 report on consumer credit, March 2011)
- In 2011, the average credit-card debt of U.S. households was $14,750, up from $2,966 in 1990 (Source: creditcards.com)
- Women are considered the #1 marketing opportunity of the next decade. Women are making almost all the money-based decisions now. 94% of home furnishings, 92% holiday buying, 91% homes, 89% choice of new bank account, 88% medical insurance. (Source: Women and Money (tuliptreepress.com/women))

The truth is that as we are looking into all the areas of our lives, searching for truth and identity, we HAVE to take the time to put money in its proper place. We must look at our attitudes about it, the role it plays in our lives and honestly assess its control over us.

First of all, is having money bad? NO!

1. God is the one who gives you money.

    a. Everything we have comes from Him.

    b. He is the one who owns everything.

    c. He generously provides for our needs.

But remember the Lord your God, for it is he who gives you the ability to produce wealth. –Deuteronomy 8:18a NIV

2. God loves to bless us.

    a. As our Father, God loves to provide the things we need.

    b. His very nature is generosity.

You parents--if your children ask for a loaf of bread, do you give them a stone instead? Or if they ask for a fish, do you give them a snake? Of course not! If you sinful people know how to give good gifts to your children, how much more will your heavenly Father give good gifts to those who ask him?

Matthew 7:9-11

Lesson Six

3. God gives to us so that we can bless others.

    a. He wants us to be generous with what He gives us.

    b. We are His hands and feet here on earth, and He will use us to bless other people financially.

    c. We are called, as His children to take care of the poor, the widow, the orphan and those who are in need.

Yes, you will be enriched so that you can give even more generously.
–2 Corinthians 9:11a

So what is the problem?

The truth is that money is one of the greatest hindrances to *contentment* in my life.

When I honestly look at how money affects my life and outlook, I have to say that it has more power over me than I would like to admit: I can become completely depressed when I can't buy what I want; I can be over the moon when I get to buy something new; I can lie awake all night long worrying about not having enough of it. All these things make it clear to me that money's control over my thoughts, actions and moods would indicate a level of influence that I wish wasn't there.

For the love of money is the root of all kinds of evil. –1 Timothy 6:10

Here are some of the ways "the love of money" leads me astray:

1. "I Gotta Have It…."

    a. The Problem:

- I become dissatisfied with what I have.
  - "These clothes are so old…."
  - "This couch is so ugly…."
  - "I hate all this stuff…."
- I am always wanting more.
  - "If I could just finish decorating my bedroom…."
  - "If I could just get some new clothes so I wouldn't feel so fat…."
  - If I could just get a few more things for the kids to play with…."

Greed has many faces, but speaks one language: the language of more.
–*Cure for the Common Life* by Max Lucado

Watch out! Be on your guard against all kinds of greed; a man's life does not consist in the abundance of his possessions.

Luke 12:15
NIV

- I have a lack of good stewardship.
  - Buying things we can't afford.
  - Not sticking to a budget.
  - Not being responsible with the finances God has entrusted to me.
  - Too much debt.

Lesson Six

> We didn't actually overspend our budget. The allocation simply fell short of our expenditure. –Keith Davis.

b. The Solution:

> Don't be <u>obsessed</u> with getting more material things. Be <u>relaxed</u> with what you have. –Hebrews 13:5 MSG

I think the key words here are *OBSESSED* and *RELAXED*

- **Obsess:** To preoccupy the mind excessively. Compulsive preoccupation with a fixed idea, often accompanied by symptoms of anxiety.
- **Relaxed:** Free from strain or tension. Easy and informal in manner.
- Ask yourself: Am I *OBSESSING* about money and things?
  - How often am I talking about "what I want to buy….?"
  - How much time do I think about new purchases?
  - Am I content with what I have, or do I always feel dissatisfied when I look at my home, clothes, car, etc.?
  - Am I being responsible with my finances, or am I spending more than I should be?
  - How often do I find myself buying things on impulse?
  - Am I disciplined in my spending, or do I find I lack control?
- Ask yourself: Do I have a *RELAXED* attitude about money?
  - How much time do I spend figuring out a way to buy something?
  - How often do my husband and I fight about my spending?
  - Can I look around my house and closet and still feel content?
  - If I can't buy something, what is my response and attitude?

I remember a day when Jeff and I were at a store, and I got it in my head that I wanted to buy the kids a little picnic table for the backyard. I had been researching them online all week long, and was very excited about a little set I had found with two benches and a little umbrella.

I showed him the adorable mini-furniture, and he looked at the price tag and said, "Do you *REALLY* think we need this?" I tried to stay calm. "Well, yeah! It's so cute and it matches our big picnic table, and it would be so fun...." I continued to run down my list of all the amazing ways this table was going to enrich our lives and the lives of our children and our children's children.

He wasn't falling for it.

"Kristie, I just don't think this is the best thing to spend our money on. We don't need it."

After a few more conversations back and forth, I finally relented. As we continued our shopping adventure, I was ... well, I guess the only way to describe it, is ... I was pouting. Putting on a really good show. In my head I was whining and complaining and feeling *VERY* sorry for myself that my husband would deprive our children of such a wonderful gift.

After about twenty minutes of this, I suddenly felt the Holy Spirit speak to my heart: "Really, Kristie?" (That's how He talks to me ☺) "Are you really going to spend the rest of the day pouting because you didn't get to buy something?" Instantly, I was embarrassed at my behavior; I was acting like a spoiled child; I didn't get what I wanted, so I was going to behave poorly. Yuck.

Our reactions to situations like this can be a great window into our hearts. This was a great moment for me to realize that I was putting *WAY* too much stock in a "*THING*." I think of that moment often, and try not to let myself become so attached to the things I want to buy.

Another way we can struggle with money is....

2. "I'm so worried about it...."

   a. The Problem:

     • My anxiety about our finances consumes my thoughts.

       - "How are we going to make it?"

       - "Where is the money going to come from?"

- "I cannot see the light at the end of the tunnel."
- Fear, stress and worry about money are our constant companions.

We bite our fingernails. We pace the floor. We lie awake at night. And all because of worry. Hour after hour, our mental fingers twist around a problem, turning it this way, then that, like a Rubik's Cube. We manipulate and postulate, desperate to solve the puzzle. And yet we seem to find few answers.

Having a Mary Heart in a Martha's World by Joanna Weaver

- It's a significant source of stress and conflict in my relationships.
  - Disagreements over how to spend money.
  - Frustration over how my spouse spends money.
  - Perhaps there's conflict with parents or friends over your constant need to borrow money.
  - Worry about not being able to afford what other people in your world afford.

I used to *DREAD* baby showers. I know it seems like a silly thing, but when Jeff and I were first married, we had very little money and it seemed like *ALL* of our friends were having babies; I truly wanted to celebrate with my friends, but after awhile, it really started to add up!

I can't tell you the amount of times I said "yes" to going in on a big gift for a friend's shower when I *KNEW* I didn't really have the money to spend. Or the times I would stand in the store for hours, totally stressed out, trying to figure out a creative gift that wouldn't cost very much money. I was too prideful to just gracefully turn down the invitation, and I was too embarrassed to be honest about our finances.

Causes us to make decisions solely based on financial reasons.
  - We are miserable in our job, but won't make changes because we fear financial insecurity.

- Your husband is miserable in his job, but feels pressure from you to maintain a certain income.

If a choice must be made between financial affluence and work which suits the temperament, talents and spiritual gifts of either man or woman, then the truly godly choice will surely be to honor our humanity and live within the framework of who we are.

A Woman's Worth by Elaine Stedman

- Holding on too tightly to money.
  - We look at money as our source of security.
  - Lacking generosity.
  - We find it difficult to share what we have.
  - We can't enjoy the blessings God has given us because we're so fearful of not having enough.

And God will generously provide for all you need. Then you will always have everything you need and plenty left over to share with others.

–2 Corinthians 9:8

b. The Solution:

- Recognize that worry about money reveals a lack of trust in God.
  - At the heart of it, we are doubting that God is watching over us.
  - We aren't sure that He will take care of our needs.
  - We doubt His provision will be there when we need it.
  - We think that our job is our provider, not God. Therefore the idea of making a much-needed change seems too risky.

Lesson Six

So I tell you, don't worry about everyday life – whether you have enough food, drink and clothes. Doesn't life consist of more than food and clothing?

Matthew 6:25-33

Look at the birds. They don't need to plant or harvest or put food in barns because your heavenly Father feeds them. And you are far more valuable to him that they are. Can all your worries add a single moment to your life? Of course not. And why worry about your clothes?

Look at the lilies and how they grow. They don't work or make their clothing, yet Solomon in all his glory was not dressed as beautifully as they are. And if God cares so wonderfully for flowers that are here today and gone tomorrow, won't he more surely care for you? You have so little faith!

So don't worry about having enough food or drink or clothing. Why be like the pagans who are so deeply concerned about these things? Your heavenly Father already knows all your needs, and he will give you all you need from day to day if you live for him and make the Kingdom of God your primary concern.

- Ask yourself:
  - Do I truly believe that God is looking out for me and my family?
  - Do I trust that He will provide everything we need?

Whoever trusts in his riches will fall. —Proverbs 11:28a NIV

  - Am I focusing on living God's purpose for me in my career, or simply looking for the security of a paycheck?
  - Am I encouraging my spouse to pursue a career that makes him happy, or I am fixated on what will bring us financial security and affluence?
  - Am I willing to give, knowing that God will bless me for my generosity?

When I am afraid, I will trust in you. —Psalm 56:3 NIV

And the last way we can struggle with money is....

3. "Gotta Get My Fix"

a. The Problem:

- Using shopping and money to fill something in my life.
  - When you're feeling bad, you go shopping to make yourself feel better.
  - When you're frustrated or upset, you distract yourself by buying things.
  - In a season of unhappiness, you numb the pain by purchasing things you don't need.
  - When you are stressed out, you give yourself a quick fix by buying something online.

Lesson Six

- Looking to spending as the source of my joy.
  - The key word here is *SOURCE*.
  - When we run to anything other than Jesus to fill us up, we are missing it.
  - The only source of *JOY* is Jesus.
  - When we try to fill ourselves up with *ANYTHING* other than Him, we constantly will be disappointed.

There I will go to the altar of God, to God – the source of all my joy.
—Psalm 43:4

- Buying things you don't need for the "*RUSH.*"

It was a bright, sunny springtime morning. As I looked outside my window, I noticed an unusual amount of traffic. Suddenly, it hit me. Today was neighborhood garage sale day. My heart started pounding. I got super excited and was suddenly filled with visions of all the wonderful treasures I was about to discover. Just think of it! Loads and loads of other people's junk that I was about to bring into my house!

I frantically started trying to get the children ready to hit the sale. All I could think of was that if we didn't hurry, everyone was going to take all the good stuff!! Of course they chose that moment to be super slow, super distracted and super *NOT* interested in going to garage sales with me. I was running around, yelling at everyone to hurry up and get out of the house, when suddenly I had a moment of clarity. (Of course, it once again was the Holy Spirit speaking correction to my oh-so-easily-swayed heart.)

Why was I so worked up? Was it really worth me making my morning so chaotic? Was it really worth me yelling at my kids? Was this really the lesson I wanted to be teaching my kids? Did I really want them to see me *FREAKING* out over buying *STUFF*?

Don't get me wrong: There's nothing wrong with enjoying shopping. There have been countless times where I have been over-the-moon thrilled because I *KNEW* God had provided something I needed, or I got a great deal for my family. That's not what I'm talking about here: When you start to love the *RUSH* you get, and start to want that *FEELING*, I would say you need to stop and give yourself a heart check.

For me, that day, I knew that I needed to stay home. No garage sales for me. I recognized the imbalance in my heart, and made a decision to discipline myself.

- Shopping with money you don't have for things you don't need:
  - clothes, shoes, jewelry
  - stuff for your children
  - buying things for your home
  - garage sales
  - online shopping
  - home Shopping Network
- Out of control spending:
  - buying things you don't need
  - having many lines of credit with no thought of the cumulative total of your debt
  - trying to stop, but continually being undisciplined when it comes to your money

Whoever loves money never has enough; whoever loves wealth is never satisfied with his income. –Ecclesiastes 5:0 NIV

Lesson Six

b. The Solution:

- Resist the urge to pacify yourself with shopping.

- Be honest about your emotions.
  - What is really upsetting me?
  - Am I bored?
  - Am I nervous?
  - Am I angry?
  - Am I feeling insecure?

- Deal with the real issues.
  - Sit down with a journal and write about what you're feeling.
  - Get some clarity and ask God for wisdom.
  - If you're upset with another person, do whatever you need to do to work through it: Forgive them, apologize to them or have the tough conversation.
  - Educate yourself: Spend some time looking at books, articles, or blogs or the topic you are dealing with.
  - Allow Jesus to comfort you, encourage you and give you wisdom and direction.

Remember your promise to me, for it is my only hope. Your promise revives me; it comforts me in all my troubles. —Psalm 119:49-50

- Discipline yourself when it comes to spending:

At the time, discipline isn't much fun. It always feels like it's going against the grain. Later, of course, it pays off handsomely, for it's the well-trained who find themselves mature in their relationship with God.

Hebrews
12:11
MSG

- stick to a budget.
  - cash only.
  - avoid impulse buying.
- Make a list
- avoid "wandering"
- avoid temptation
- freeze your credit card in a block of ice so it has to defrost before you can use it ☺

Actually, I don't have a sense of needing anything personally. I've learned by now to be quite content whatever my circumstances. I'm just as happy with little as with much, with much as with little. I've found the recipe for being happy whether full or hungry, hands full or empty. Whatever I have, wherever I am, I can make it through anything in the One who makes me who I am.

Phillipians
4:11-13
MSG

GROUP DISCUSSION QUESTIONS

- What are some ways the "I Gotta Have It" mentality affects you and your family?
- Discuss some of your worries about finances.
- Share some of the tips you have found helpful in dealing with:
  - Budgets
  - Disciplining your spending
  - Resisting the urge to find security in your finances instead of in God

Lesson Six

GOING DEEPER

First of all, take some time to remember how God has taken care of you financially. Think of the blessings in your life. Remember the times that He has supernaturally provided for you. **Write out your memories here and remind yourself of His faithfulness to you.**

He causes us to remember his wonderful works. How gracious and merciful is our Lord! –Psalm 111:4

Think of some ways where you struggle with the "I Gotta Have It" syndrome.

What are some ways you feel dissatisfied with what you have?

What are some areas you struggle with wanting "more?" List some specifics.

Stewardship is simply managing what has been given to you. God has given you everything you have. How do you feel you are managing these things? What are some specific ways you are being a good steward? What are some areas you should work on?

Remember the verse we looked at earlier:

Don't be obsessed with getting more material things. Be relaxed with what you have. —Hebrews 13:5 MSG

What are some things you are "obsessing" about?

How can you be more "relaxed" with what you have?

Money can be a significant source of worry and anxiety. What are some things you are worrying about in your finances?

How is anxiety about finances affecting your relationships?

How do you like your job? Is it rewarding? Is it fulfilling? Do you feel like you are right where God wants you? If not, what is keeping you there?

If you're married, ask yourself the same questions regarding your spouse's job. Is he happy? Is he passionate about what he's doing? Are you supporting him in his career choices? Do you think he feels pressure from you to maintain a certain income level and lifestyle? **Write out your thoughts here.**

If God is speaking to your heart about some decisions you have been making solely out of financial reasons instead of seeking God, write out a prayer of surrender and some action steps you need to take.

Are you generous? What was the last thing you gave away? Is God speaking to your heart about letting go of your tight hold on your money? **Write out your thoughts here.**

List one practical way in which God is calling you to be generous.

Do you trust God with your finances? Do you believe that He is going to take care of you? **Write out your honest thoughts and fears in this area.**

Are you looking to money or things as the source of your joy? Honestly look at your shopping/spending habits. Are you numbing your pain or insecurity by spending? **Specifically describe your struggles in this area.**

Lesson Six

How is your level of debt? Are you spending more than you are making? Ask God to give you specific wisdom in this area. Specifically what do you need to change? **What practical steps can you take to get yourself out of debt?**

Honestly evaluate your reasons for overspending. What is really going on? What are you dealing with on the inside?

Godliness with contentment is great gain. —1 Timothy 6:6 NIV

Help! I'm Lost

LOSING YOURSELF IN YOUR ROLES

> *I was not developing individual taste or initiative – I was simply absorbing the personalities of those about me and letting their tastes and interests dominate me.* –Eleanor Roosevelt

It seems an all too common occurrence. You start a new job. You meet a new guy. You have a baby. You get involved in a new ministry. You begin investing in your career. You pour yourself into your relationship. You throw yourself into your new role as a mother.

But somewhere along the way, something happens. For one reason or another, you begin to define yourself by these roles and relationships. You invest so much of who you are into being the very best wife, mother, employee, girlfriend, daughter you can be. And one day, you wake up and realize that you have lost yourself in the process.

All your time, energy, and identity are firmly embedded in the lives of other people's expectations and needs. Your time is dictated by what everyone else asks of you. Your energy is spent on behalf of what everyone else needs. Your identity is simply what you are to other people.

Why do we, as women lose ourselves so easily?

1. We're givers by nature

   a. As women, we are naturally nurturing.

   • We truly care about the people in our world.

   • There's something instinctively in us that wants to make sure that everyone's ok.

   b. We want to do our best at the roles we have.

   • We are also driven, focused, and desire to be successful.

   • We want to make sure we do things well.

   • We feel responsibility and a sense of ownership in our jobs and families.

c. When we love something, we want to pour ourselves into it with everything we have.

- Out of our sincere love and affection, we simply give.
- It's a part of who we are as women to love deeply.

2. A desire to please.

a. Really wanting to make our bosses, spouses and children happy.

b. We want to please other people.

c. We have a fear of confrontation.

- We are afraid of saying no.
- We don't want to upset someone.
- Instead of making decisions on what is God's best for us, we make decisions on what will make other people happy.

d. We need to feel validated and affirmed.

- We all want to feel appreciated and loved.
- Sometimes our desire for this can cause us to pour too much into other people, looking for them to affirm us.

3. Some of us have a tendency towards dependence on other people.

a. Perhaps your childhood was such that you were taught to be dependent instead of independent.

b. Maybe you've become accustomed to being needed, and over time have come to rely on it for validation.

c. Any number of personality factors, temperament issues, and life experiences can find us in a season where we have lost our sense of self.

What are some common ways we lose ourselves?

1. We lose ourselves in our relationships.

    a. Boyfriends, husbands, friends, parents, siblings… the list goes on and one.

    b. We absorb the life of people we are close to instead of forging out our own place in the world.

When Jeff and I were planning our wedding, the minister asked us an interesting question. We were discussing the unity candle, and he asked us if we were going to blow out our individual candles after we lit the one in the middle. I was curious as to why that would even be an issue. He said, "Some people blow out their individual candle because they are symbolizing that they are leaving behind the person that they were, and joining themselves wholly to their spouse. The other school of thought is that you leave your personal candles lit after you light the unity candle simply because you don't stop being an individual just cause you're married."

Interesting thought then, VERY interesting thought now.

Simply because I see how very easy it is to lose your unique sense of self once you get married. Not only in marriage, it's easy to lose your sense of self in any close, intimate relationship. Trying to be who your parents want you to be. Trying to be like your sister. Trying to be the kid of girl your boyfriend says he has ALWAYS wanted to marry, even though you are nothing like that!

Why do we do this?

    c. We are trying to create the fairy tale.

- We try to become something in our imagination.
- We desperately want a relationship to work, so we try to become what we think the other person wants us to be.
- We allow our expectations to change us into something we're not.

It wasn't Lance [my husband] saying, "You should be like this" or "Do this," she says. It wasn't him making a mandate and me being a mouse. It was me trying to emulate whatever I thought would be the perfect wife or the perfect mother…

Kristen
Armstrong

Lesson Seven

d. We don't take ownership of our choices.

- Sometimes we're not sure of who we are or who we want to be, and so it's easier to let someone define it for us.

- Perhaps you were never taught how to make choices for yourself. It can become difficult to assert your opinions and wants when you've never been allowed to make decisions for yourself.

> *A common boundary problem is disowning our choices and trying to lay the responsibility for them on someone else.*
>
> —*Boundaries* by Dr. Henry Cloud and Dr. John Townsend

- Not wanting to be responsible. The weight of making a decision is a heavy load to carry. Sometimes its easy to just let others make decisions for you.

- Fear of making the wrong decisions.

Coming Up for Air by Margaret Becker

I wonder if it's been easier to wrap myself up in expectation – other people's expectations of what my life should stand for, what it should look like – than it would have been to determine these things for myself. There is a certain degree of safety in relying on other people to do the determining for you.

If you can't fulfill it, it is much easier to blame it on the "system" or the "expectation" than it is to admit that it was you, and you alone, who set the standard for yourself – and, perhaps, who failed it. It's easier, I think, to be safe than it is to understand your own personal life's infrastructure. It's easier to not know than it is to labor and learn.

Another common problem is that…

2. We lose ourselves in our children.

After putting her children to bed, a mother changed into clean slacks and a fresh blouse and proceeded to wash her hair. As she heard the children getting more and more rambunctious, her tolerance grew thin. Finally, she had had enough and stormed into their room, putting them back to bed with severe warnings. While leaving the room, she overheard her three-year-old say with a shaky voice, "Who was 'that'?" –Anonymous

Being a mother has unequivocally changed my life. I don't look at anything the same way I did before I had children. From the moment they entered my life, they had my heart in a way that I didn't know was possible. Suddenly nothing else seemed important. I knew, in a split second, that I would give myself totally and completely to them in every way.

Making the decision to have a child – it's momentous. It is to decide forever to have your heart walking around outside your body. –Elizabeth Stone

A new baby most certainly takes over your life: You sleep when they let you sleep. You get up when they get up. You feed them when they're hungry. You change them when they're dirty. In essence, you do whatever they tell you to do.

So it's easy to see how, out of necessity, we start motherhood in a pattern of revolving our life around our children. But what was meant to be a temporary season, for most of us, becomes a way of life.

It is so easy to lose ourselves in motherhood!

Even if we think it will never happen to us, most of us at some point or another realize that we have ceased to have any kind of a life outside of our children.

Why is that bad?

    a. It's not good for your kids.

- It teaches them that the world revolves around them.
- We don't give them the tools to learn where they fit in social situations… a skill vitally important as they get older.
- We put a responsibility on them that they are not equipped to carry.

Children shouldn't have to look out for their parents, parents look out for their children. −2 Corinthians 12:14 MSG

- We put the weight of OUR happiness on their shoulders

Some children were born to take care of their parents. They didn't sign up for this duty; they inherited it. Today we call these people "codependent." Early in life they learned they were responsible for their parents, who were stuck in childish patterns of irresponsibility.

Boundries by Dr. Henry Cloud & Dr. John Townsend

- We fail to teach them independence:
  - we're always picking up after them;
  - we cover their mistakes;
  - we solve all their problems.

b. It's not good for your marriage.

- Neglect your marriage for the sake of the children can cause BIG trouble.
- Your marriage should be the center of your family structure.

For those of you who are married, the secret to raising happy, healthy children is to give more attention to the marriage than you give to the children.

–Six Point Plan For Raising Happy Children by John Rosemond

- If you don't invest in your marriage now, there will be nothing left when the kids are gone.

c. It's not good for you.

- We will not grow in our faith when we constantly look for fulfillment in our children – instead of looking to God to fill the longings in our heart.
- If we are "overly involved" with our children's lives, we will be tempted to take on things that are not ours to take on.

Problems arise when boundaries of responsibility are confused. We are to <u>love</u> *one another, not be one another. I can't feel your feelings for you. I can't think for you. I can't behave for you. I can't work through the disappointment that limits bring for you. In short, I can't grow for you; only you can. Likewise, you can't grow for me.*

Boundries by Dr. Henry Cloud & Dr. John Townsend

- You need to maintain your own sense of "personhood"

Lesson Seven

Another temptation many of us face is ...

3. We lose ourselves in our jobs.

A few years ago, my father-in-law, John Kerr, told Jeff and I that he had a new idea for a book. It was called "Lose Your Job, Find Your Life." The premise was that so many of us have our identity and worth so wrapped up in success, achievement, and accomplishment. We don't have any sense of personhood outside of what we are achieving.

John is the absolute opposite of that. He has been a pastor and missionary for his entire adult life. He has multiple master's degrees as well as his PhD. He is a grandfather, father, and husband. But he is first and foremost the most self-contained, confident, and grounded person I know. He could give a flying flip what anyone thinks about him. He lives his life to please God, and is not at all caught in the trap of success and stature. He humbly walks with his God, and that's it.

OH, that I had that assurance. I have spent many, many years trying to learn that delicate art. I am easily, easily lost inside any kind of work that I am doing. Whether it's an actual job that pays me something, or an area I am volunteering in, or a project I am working on; I am pretty much an "all or nothing" kind of gal.

I feel ownership and responsibility and I always want to go the extra mile. Unfortunately that means that I can become totally wrapped up in whatever I am doing at the moment, and can find myself lost in the process. I have learned the hard way that this kind of drive can very quickly lead you into all kinds of trouble.

    a. We begin to define ourselves by our successes and failures.
- When things are going good – we feel great.
- When things are going bad – we feel horrible.
- We are at the mercy of our performance.

    b. We make choices based on achievement instead of living to please God.
- When we NEED to be successful to feel good about ourselves, we lose all perspective.
- We blindly move toward what will grant us more perceived success instead of looking at the big picture of what God is asking of us.

    c. You will exhaust yourself trying to gain your identity in what you are do.
- It's a dangerous trap.
- You become dependent on the praise and adulation that comes from success, and therefore you're driven to get more and more.

- You will keep spinning your wheels faster and faster at the detriment of yourself, your family, and those around you.

d. We find that we might stay in a place that is really unhealthy for us because we've become so entwined in that role for our identity, that we feel paralyzed to step away from it.

- Even if we KNOW we should.

- Even if we KNOW God is asking us to.

- Even if we KNOW its become out of balance and unhealthy.

- The fear of being without it can cause us to remain in a place we shouldn't be.

So, how do we overcome this? How do we guard ourselves from becoming lost in our roles?

1. Live to please God.

a. God must come first.

- Mentally making the shift that everything we are and everything we do HAS to be rooted and established in Him.

Christ is the visible image of the invisible God.

He existed before anything was created and is supreme over all creation, for through him God created everything in the heavenly realms and on earth. He made the things we can see and the things we can't see— such as thrones, kingdoms, rulers, and authorities in the unseen world. Everything was created through him and for him. He existed before anything else, and he holds all creation together. Christ is also the head of the church, which is his body. He is the beginning, supreme over all who rise from the dead. So he is first in everything.

Colossians 1:15-18

- Everything we are is for His purpose.
- Everything we do is for His glory.
- Our selfish ambition and desire to please others must be pushed down and replaced be a desire to please God.

The very essence of sin is putting something finite before God. No one can serve two masters. Whatever honor and devotion we offer God is meaningless if at the same time there is a rival to him in our loyalty and affection. Actually, the rival to God is not others, but the self using others to sustain a sense of worth.

A Woman's Worth by Elaine Stedman

b. Stop looking to the people in your world for approval and security.

Cursed is the one who trusts in man, who depends on flesh for his strength, and whose heart turns away from the Lord. –Jeremiah 17:5

- Resist the temptation to find your value and worth in the way other people view you.
- No human being was meant to carry the weight of your security.
- You must ruthlessly rid yourself of the tendency to define yourself by the roles you play and instead define yourself by who you are in Christ.

c. We need to seek to know the heart of God and what His view of us is.

- Ask God to give you a revelation of who He made you to be.
- The unique gifts He gave to you when He created you.

You made all the delicate, inner parts of my body and knit me together in my mother's womb. Thank you for making me so wonderfully complex! Your workmanship is marvelous—how well I know it. –Psalm 139:13-14

- Not just the things you DO, but who you ARE.
  - Maybe He made you creative.
  - Maybe He gave you the gift of compassion.
  - Maybe He made you intellectual and to love learning.
  - Maybe He made you super sensitive toward the needs of others.
  - Maybe He made you funny.
  - Maybe He made you athletic.
  - Maybe He made you enjoy nature.
  - Maybe He made you meticulous and detail oriented.
- All of these things can be USED in the roles you play, but your individuality and identity are the unique combination of all these things simply in their organic state.

2. Embrace the exceptional aspects who God created you to be.

a. He made you unique.

- There is NO ONE other than you who has the combination of personality, skills, appearance and outlook you do.
- And that specific marriage of gifts in you will allow you to have a completely individual perspective on the world.
- A perspective that God created, because He wanted that view existent in the world!

But now, this is what the Lord says – he who created you, O Jacob, he who formed you, O Israel; "Fear not, for I have redeemed you; I have summoned you by name; you are mine.

Isaiah 43:1
NIV

Lesson Seven

b. He has a purpose for your life that requires YOU to be YOU.

- God needs you to be exactly who He made you to be.
- There is no need to try and change yourself into what you think other people want you to be.
- He created you just the way He wanted!

God, in his faithfulness, is changing me. But I remain an extrovert. In fact, instead of making me into someone else, he is making me more me.

–*Captivating* by John & Staci Eldridge

c. Be secure in who God made you to be.

3. Begin to OWN your life as an individual.

a. Own **your** faith.

- Take personal responsibility for your spiritual growth and condition.
- Don't look to your significant other, your children, your friends or even your pastor for your spiritual growth. It is YOUR job to nurture your relationship with Jesus.
- Be diligent about cultivating your individual relationship with Jesus.
- Keep some things just between you and God. Learn to have a space in you world that is simply you and Him.

Mary kept all these things to herself, holding them dear, deep within herself.

–Luke 2:19 MSG

We enter and we exit life alone. The personal intimacy of our relationship with God cannot and must not be mediated or interpolated by any other person.

—*A Woman's Identity* by Elaine Stedman

b. Value **your** feelings.

- Your feelings are your responsibility.
- Don't expect others to take care of your needs for fulfillment, comfort, and security.
- Don't continually disregard your feelings; God gave them to you for a reason!
- Learn to honor what you are feeling, and bring it to Jesus and let Him help you work through them.
- Cultivate a sense of personal ownership and responsibility.

c. Take responsibility for **your** behaviors.

- Constantly bring your behaviors and attitudes before Jesus. Repent if you need to repent. If something needs to be made right, then make it right.
- Make decisions that need to be made. Don't wait for someone to make them for you.
- Speak up when you need to speak up.
- Own your choices, decisions, and the direction of your life.

d. Be honest about what you really think or want.

- Don't edit yourself – with yourself.

I am amazed at my capacity to even stop myself from THINKING a certain way because I think someone wouldn't approve of it. I will even be writing in my journal, expressing my frustrations, and then quickly cross it out and write the "spiritual version" or the thing I know I SHOULD say. But I'm learning that this kind of editing myself simply keeps me from really owning my own thoughts or feelings. I'm realizing that feeling a certain way doesn't mean I have to instantly turn into a selfish mess. Defining what's going on in my heart is the first step towards authenticity. After all, the first thing Jesus asks us to do it CONFESS. Bring it to the surface, shine light on it, and then bring it under HIS Lordship and do with it whatever He tells you to.

- Force yourself to not just say what you think people WANT to hear.
- Be diligent about examining your own feelings and honestly articulate them.
- This isn't about being selfish, or demanding your own way.
- Truly authentic relationships HAVE to be able to work through issues with honesty. You cannot honestly work through something if you don't honestly express where you are coming from.

The Woman Behind the Mask by Jan Coleman

Like me, you may have been piling on the masks for years, and you've played so many roles you're not sure which one is you. Becoming an authentic woman means...going beneath the persona to find the real woman, discover your original voice and tempo...find the parts of your personality that you despised and suppressed. WE have to be open emotionally and spiritually for the Lord to define who we are.

4. Have a life outside your family and job.

Ok. I can hear you all right now gasping in horror at this statement. "What are you saying, Kristie! That I should have a secret crazy life outside of my family!" Calm down my friends. I am not talking about living a double life.

But there is something very healthy about having things that you do JUST FOR YOU. Things that replenish you, inspire you, and bring you joy outside of the main relationships in your family. And this is ESPECIALLY important if you are losing yourself in your job. You must find ways to define yourself outside of the context of your work.

    a. If you're trying to live your life vicariously through your husband or boyfriend, instead of purposefully owning and enjoying your own life, you will suffocate the relationship.

b. You must find something you enjoy outside of being a mom.

- Be diligent about taking time away from your kids to focus on your friendships, hobbies, and things you enjoy.
- If you simply live your life through what your kids are doing, you will not have the balance and perspective to parent them well. You're too wrapped up in it.

"So, Paul, how often do you try to get out?"

"Any time I can. Probably about two nights a week and one afternoon on the weekend."

"What do you do at those times?" I asked Meredith.

"Well, I wait for him to come home. I miss him very much."

"Don't you have something you want to do for yourself?"

"No. My family is my life. I live for them. I hate it when they are gone and we can't have time together."

—*Boundaries* by Dr. Henry Cloud and Dr. John Townsend

c. Be diligent about having a life outside of your job:

- begin and end your day with something just for you
- spend time with your friends
- take the time to do things you enjoy
- make sure you are taking time off

Lesson Seven

5. Remember who you are!

   a. You are God's girl.

   b. You are a unique individual.

   c. You are a beautiful woman.

   d. You have intelligence and wisdom to offer the world.

   e. You have special gifts and talents to use.

One of my favorite authors, Mrs. Elaine Stedman wrote a beautiful book called "A Woman's Worth" in the 1970's as a response to the women's liberation movement. She was seeking to address women's search for identity and equality, which was becoming a very socially dynamic discussion. The church was struggling to find a Biblical voice on the subject, and I think Mrs. Stedman's perspective was profound in teaching us to balance the individual and strong spirit God created in women, and a healthy understanding of our place in our homes, jobs, churches, and society. Her conclusion was that we simply need to find our value, worth, position and identity solely in Christ. Here is my favorite except from her book.

I am God's woman. He made me. I accept my unique design without resentment, knowing that God's intention for me is loving and redemptive.

A multitude of complicated hereditary and cultural factors have combined to make me what I am, but in the end nothing and no one can thwart God's redemptive plan for me. He chose me before the foundations of the earth, destined me to be conformed to his image, and has provided me with every spiritual resource I need to be a fulfilled person and to relate to others with security and joy.

Nothing I can do – or not do – will change God's value system; only the righteousness of his son is acceptable before him, and he sees me in Christ. That frees me to be what I am: God's woman. That is my identity. I am his and he is mine. I am available to him, and he is available to me. This is the source of my security, and this is what frees me from the need to use others to validate me as a person.

A Woman's Worth by Elaine Stedman

GROUP DISCUSSION QUESTIONS

- Why do you think its so easy for us to lose ourselves in our roles?

- Share a specific area in which you are tempted to find your identity in someone or something outside of Christ?

- What is one thing you like to do outside of your family or job?

GOING DEEPER

Many of us fight the temptation to lose our sense of self, and instead get lost inside our roles as wife, mom, employer, daughter, employee, and countless other things. But God wants each of us to live the life He designed and planned for us!

Take some time to honestly answer the questions below.

Is there an area of your life where you have been pouring yourself and you are becoming invisible in the process?

Lesson Seven

Lets look at your relationships. How are you doing at maintaining boundaries in your relationships? Are you maintaining your personal sense of self? **Write out your thoughts.**

How about your relationship with your children? Are you living your life vicariously through them? Are you overly involved in their relationships and experiences, taking them on as your own?

What is your relationship with work? Do you tend to get out of balance when it comes to your job? Are you seeing ambition, greed, or selfishness creeping in when you look at your career?

Are you struggling with a desire to please other people? Allow the Holy Spirit to shine His light into your heart and reveal areas where your desire to make other people happy is out of balance. **Write out your thoughts.**

Is there an area where you need to confront someone, and yet you are unable to do so because you haven't maintained an appropriate boundary? Ask God to give you the courage to speak up and address the conflict. Practice that conversation right now. Write out what you need to say to that person and then ask God to give you the wisdom as to when and how to have the REAL conversation. (You can do it baby!!!!)

Are you defining yourself by your successes or failures? **Write out some of your struggles in this area.**

Let's begin looking at ways you can gain back your God given identity.

Determine to live your life to please God and not others. Write out a prayer of commitment right now to live your life to honor God.

What are some ways you can begin to own your faith? Think of some personal steps you need to take to begin to grow your PERSONAL relationship with Jesus.

God made you a unique individual. What is different about you? What are your distinct characteristics? Name some things that define who you are as a person.

You are responsible for your feelings. In what ways have you not valued or honored your feelings? What are some ways that you can take responsibility for your emotions?

In the same way, you need to take responsibility for your actions. What are some ways you have been avoiding the ownership of your behavior? Blaming other people? Avoiding needed decisions? Riding the coattails of other people's decisions?

List three things that you need to act on in order to take responsibility for your faith, feelings, and actions. **Write out specific steps and follow through with those this week.**

Now its time to get a life! ☺ What are some things you would enjoy doing JUST FOR YOU? Not related to your family, work, or responsibilities. Just for you. **Write them out here and commit to doing one or two of them this week.**

But blessed is the man who trusts in the Lord, whose confidence is in him. He will be like a tree planted by the water that sends out its roots by the stream. It does not fear when heat comes; its leaves are always green. It has no worries in a year of drought and never fails to bear fruit. —Jeremiah 17:7

Give It a Rest

HONORING A SABBATH

He that can take rest is greater than he that can take cities.
—Benjamin Franklin

What is a Sabbath?

Remember to observe the Sabbath day by keeping it holy. Six days a week are set apart for your daily duties and regular work, but the seventh day is a day of rest dedicated to the Lord your God. On that day no one in your household may do any kind of work. This includes you, your sons and daughters; your male and female servants, your livestock and any foreigners living among you. For in six days the Lord made the heavens, the earth, the sea and everything in them; then he rested on the seventh day. That is why the Lord blessed the Sabbath day and set it apart as holy.

Exodus
20:8-11

- The word "Sabbath" comes from a Hebrew verb meaning "**to cease**, stop, desist; to come to an end, rest."
- It's one of the **Ten Commandments** (listed in Exodus 20).
- Traditionally observed on the seventh day of the week (Saturday) but historically has moved to Sundays by Christians to celebrate the day Jesus was raised from the dead.
- In Bible times, the land was to observe a Sabbath; it was to be worked for six years and rested during the seventh year.

- In the Old Testament, the penalty for breaking the Sabbath law was *death*.

Basically, a Sabbath is a day in which we take the time to rest and worship. We step away from our normal routine and work, and instead allow ourselves time to reflect, connect with our families and rejuvenate our bodies.

Okay, confession time; Although I love the idea of a Sabbath, it's really easy to make excuses as to why it just doesn't work for *ME*. Surely, when God was talking about a Sabbath, he couldn't have meant me! Doesn't he know how busy I am??!!

Why do we find it so hard to keep a Sabbath?

1. We don't think it applies to us.

a. "It doesn't fit into my season of life."
- "My kids won't let me have a Sabbath."
- "I am *WAY* too busy to have a whole day not accomplishing anything."
- "There are just too many responsibilities in my life right now."
- "I'll retire in a few year and *THEN* I'll rest."

b. "I really don't need that much rest."
- "I'm a high-capacity person."
- "I function better when I just keep going."
- "I enjoy my work – so it's kind of like I'm resting all the time!"

c. "That's a luxury I can't afford."
- "I would *LOVE* to have a Sabbath … but I just can't."
- "It sounds pretty nice, but there's no way I could make that work for my life."

2. It feels indulgent.

a. "I just can't relax."
- "I have too much to worry about."
- "I get bored too easily."
- "I feel like I'm shirking my responsibilities."

b. "There are too many things that need to be done."
- "I just can't justify the time when I have so much to do"
- "If I don't do it, it's just not going to happen."

c. "I feel lazy."
  - "It feels like something that spoiled rich people do."
  - "I just can't get over the guilt."
  - "I was raised to be a hard worker...."

3. We can't fit it in.

  a. We have too much on our plates:
  - Out of control work schedules.
  - We've overcommitted so now we just have to keep running.
  - An inability to say no has bogged us down with too many activities.

  b. Our family schedule won't allow for it:
  - My kids are involved in sports.
  - We have too many extra-curricular activities.
  - We are all involved in our own things, and therefore the cumulative total is overwhelming our family calendar.

  c. We're already committed to other things:
  - "We have sports commitments...."
  - "We have family commitments...."
  - "We have work commitments...."

4. We don't trust God:

  a. With our finances;
  - "I have to work, or there won't be any money."
  - "I need the overtime pay."
  - "My boss would never go for it and I could lose my job."

  b. With our time;
  - "I must do this today."
  - "I won't have any other time this week."
  - "I just can't afford to waste that much time."

Lesson Eight

c. With our schedules.

- "I am better at arranging my schedule than you are, God."
- "These are all things we *HAVE* to be involved in."
- "There's just nothing that we can eliminate!"

But the truth is:

1. The Sabbath was meant for *YOU*.

a. You are not disqualified because you have a lot to do.

b. God designed the Sabbath to assure you a time of rest every week.

c. You *NEED* it:

- Your body needs it.
- Your emotions need it.
- Your family needs it.

2. You need to recognize that it's God's order for you.

a. There is no need to feel guilty.

- God designed your body.
- He knows what you need in order to maintain health, wholeness and balance
- It's His protection for your mind, body and spirit.

b. Actually embrace it as a gift.

- It can become a refuge for you in a crazy, crazy life.
- Look at it as a way your Heavenly Father is protecting you.

c. It's God's permission for you to stop!

- It is a demonstration of His care for you.

Something about the beauty and the kindness and the concreteness of it all pierced my self-sufficiency and melted the hardness of my activism; all I wanted to do was fall down and worship a God who would think to give us such a gift. All I could do was weep at the beauty of these truths and symbolic actions, weep because so few of us — and least of all I — are courageous enough to live in this beautiful way. —Sacred Rhythms by Ruth Hayley Barton

3. It's really a matter of obedience.

  a. God has told you to do it.

  - We don't look at any of the other Ten Commandments and think they are optional for us.

  - When God tells us to do something, it is simply our job as His children to obey Him.

  b. We need to fit our lives *AROUND* a Sabbath, not the other way around.

  - You need to be purposeful about making a Sabbath a reality in your life.

  - You need to rearrange and reorder your life in order to honor this commandment.

  c. If you are limiting your activities to the things God wants you to do, then a Sabbath will fit into His plan.

So, God's rest is there for people to enter. But those who formerly heard the good news failed to enter because they disobeyed God. —Hebrews 4:6

Lesson Eight

4. It forces us to recognize who's in charge.

    a. God is the one who provides our finances.

    b. God is the one who helps me with my daily life.

    c. God is the one who orders my steps every day.

God's promise of entering his place of rest still stands, so we ought to tremble with fear that some of you might fail to get there. For this Good News - that God has prepared a place of rest - has been announced to us just as it was to them. But it did them no good because they didn't believe what God had told them.

Hebrews 4:1, 2

Practical Ideas For Keeping A Sabbath:

Have you heard of the phrase: "The Spirit of the Law vs. The Letter of the Law?" The premise of the idiom is this: You can either follow strict guidelines, rule by rule, or you can understand the spirit behind the law and honor it in the most meaningful way possible for you.

When we talk about observing a Sabbath, it's important to realize that MY day of rest might be different from the way YOU feel led to observe it. God is an individual God, and He will guide you as to the best way you can rest. If we get stuck in a bunch of rules and regulations and miss the heart of what God is providing for us, we will not experience the true intent of the Sabbath.

I am going to give you some guidelines and examples that will hopefully help you get some ideas as to how to create a meaningful Sabbath for you.

1. Your Sabbath should include:

    a. Spending some personal time with God;

- talking to God
- listening to what He says to you
- reading the Bible
- spending some time in worship
- finding some solitude

    b. Spend some time doing things you enjoy.

- hobbies
- nature
- gardening
- sports
- cooking
- reading
- pampering
- enjoying creation

How simple it truly is, the connection of God's creation with God's creation. My spirit to His sea. My eyes to His sun. My toes to His sand. My mind to His intricate designs in the hermit crabs, in the palm leaves, in the veined stone. It was all meant to be. My eyes were made to behold, to appreciate, His creation.

Coming Up for Air by Margaret Becker

Lesson Eight

c. Spend some time with the people you love.
- Visit with people who are significant to you.
- Reconnect with your family and friends after a long week at work.
- Include your kids in part of your Sabbath:
  - play games
  - go for family walks or bike rides
  - read to them
  - do family activities

Believe it or not, my burnout stemmed from the fact I did not have enough time with my kids. I did not want time away. I wanted time to read to my 4 year-old and hear about their friends and watch a good tearjerker with my teen ... Sometimes our burnout is not because we are moms but because with all the other things ... taxi, cook, teacher, janitor, maid, nurse we lose our chance to be moms. Yes, those chores are a big part of being a mom but there is something even more important. That primal need to be close to our children and cuddle. That is the best rejuvenator there is.

Taking Care of the Me in Mommy by Lisa Welchel

One thing that Jeff and I have done is to have an alternative Sabbath from one another. Because we have small children and it's difficult for us to really rest with the responsibilities that come from little kids, we decided that Jeff's Sabbath would be on Mondays (his day off) and mine would be on Saturdays. We would trade kid duties so that he would be able to really enjoy a day of relaxing and I could do the same thing on another day. I have also learned to be mindful of expecting Jeff to simply accomplish my "honey do" list on his day off; I need to allow him to spend his day doing the things that will replenish him, not simply having him do all the things I want him to do.

If we commit ourselves to creating an umbrella of safety over our marriage, we will have a shelter under which we can relax and openly and intimately enjoy our life together. Our relationship becomes a sanctuary, a safe harbor, a place we long to come home to.

—*The DNA of Relationships for Couples* by Dr. Greg Smalley & Dr. Robert S. Paul

d. Spend some time resting your body:

- take a nap

- take a bath

- take a walk

- lay around a bit ☺

2. **Some ideas of what "not" to do on your Sabbath**

NOTE: These ideas are very subjective; ask God to show you the things you need to refrain from.

a. Work.

- What does that mean for you?

- Your "paid" job.

- Worry about work.

- Mentally working.

- Your household chores.

- Large household projects.

So there is a special rest still waiting for the people of God. For all who enter into God's rest will find rest from their labors, just as God rested after creating the world. Let us do our best to enter that place of rest.

—Hebrews 4:9-10

b. Unplugging:
- phone
- emails
- computer
- TV

c. Shopping.
- Helps with my materialism struggles.
- Forces me to explore other hobbies and interests.
- Helps me avoid finding joy and fulfillment in money.

Yet, true religion with contentment is great wealth. After all, we didn't bring anything with us when we came into the world, and we certainly cannot carry anything with us when we die. So if we have enough food and clothing, let us be content.

1 Timothy 6:6-8

So, God set another time for entering His place of rest, and that time is today.

–Hebrews 4:7

Group Discussion Questions

- In reference to why we don't keep the Sabbath, which of the reasons discussed today do you most relate?

  - I cannot do it in my current season of life.
  - I feel lazy and self-indulgent.
  - Too busy to fit it in.
  - Trust issues with God.

- What does "resting from work" mean for you?

- What are some activities you would enjoy doing on your Sabbath?

Going Deeper

Why do you think it's so easy to overlook this commandment to "remember the Sabbath?"

Lesson Eight

What are some of the reasons you find it difficult to honor a Sabbath?

What are some specific ways you could take steps to involve a weekly day of rest into your life?

What are some things you would enjoy doing on your Sabbath?

What are some things you think God is asking you to refrain from doing on your day of rest?

What spiritual insight do you think you will gain from faithfully honoring this day?

Make a specific plan as to how you are going to incorporate this spiritual discipline into your weekly routine.

Remember to observe the Sabbath day by keeping it holy. Six days a week are set apart for your daily duties and regular work, but the seventh day is a day of rest dedicated to the Lord your God. —Exodus 20:8

The Search for Me

CPSIA information can be obtained
at www.ICGtesting.com
Printed in the USA
FSOW02n0327170516
20504FS

9 780578 081991